D0456742

CHILDREN OF TRAUMA

CHILDREN OF TRAUMA

Rediscovering Your Discarded Self

JANE MIDDELTON-MOZ

Health Communications, Inc.
Deerfield Beach, Florida

Jane Middelton-Moz
Seattle, Washington

Library of Congress Cataloging-in-Publication Data

Middelton-Moz, Jane
  Children of trauma.

  Bibliography: p.
  1. Adult child abuse victims — Mental health.
  2. Self-care, Health.   I. Title.
RC569.5.C55M53   1989   616.85'82   88-31971
ISBN 1-55874-014-7

Copyright ©1989 Jane Middelton-Moz
ISBN 1-55874-014-7

All rights reserved. No part of this book may be reproduced or
transmitted in any form or by any means, electronic or mechanical,
including photocopying, recording or by any information storage and
retrieval system, without written permission of the publisher, except
where permitted by law.

Printed in the United States of America

Cover Illustrations and Design by Reta Thomas

Published by: Health Communications, Inc.
             3201 S.W. 15th Street
             Deerfield Beach, Florida 33442

ACKNOWLEDGMENTS

The completion of this book is an occasion for celebration. It gives me the opportunity to acknowledge the tremendous support, clinical gifts and heart gifts of many individuals, including gifted clinicians and artists, who have added to my growth as a clinician and writer, those individuals who have supported me personally and those who have worked with me on the manuscript:

Lorie Dwinell, my co-author in *After the Tears* and a valued friend and peer, for her Introduction to *Children of Trauma*, and for the hours of personal support and clinical discussions that led to the conception and birth of this book.

Susan Arthur Harris, a valued, special friend, for the gifts of her artistic talents in the creation of the powerful and sensitive photographs that begin each chapter and for being the person she is.

Glenna Ward, my sister-in-law, friend, and support, for her long hours at the word processor, lengthy supportive discussions that followed each draft, and for her warmth and caring patience.

Michael Miller, my extremely talented editor, for his gift with words and consistent help and advice.

Pat Conroy, Rusty Berkus, Nanci Presley-Holley, Brook, Anna Latimer, Kelly Craig, J. Danielson, Barbara Huston, Don Nelsson and Ruth Kane for the poems and prose that have provided much of the heart learning in *Children of Trauma.*

Kenneth Carter, Ph.D., for first sparking my interest in psychology and clinical work.

Roger Straus, Ph.D., for being a valuable early mentor for me in the field.

Diane Laut, my office manager, for loving support, patience, and for providing organization in my daily life.

Jesse and Benjamin Harris for their assistance in the artwork.

Wynn Bloch, Jill Troy, Kathy Munson, Betty Geisay, Janet Hews, Anna Latimer, Jeffrey Middelton, Kate Grutz and Pat Hammerle for providing extremely valuable clinical and editorial feedback and input in writing and developing the concepts in the manuscript.

Rudolph Moz for long hours of clinical discussion and valuable input and feedback through the process of writing and development.

Shawn, Jason, Damien and Forrest Middelton for long hours of support, discussion and valuable suggestions, and Damien Middelton for his helpful graphics.

Erik Erikson, Yael Danieli, Karen Horney, Dan Dodson, D.W. Winnicott, Selma Fraiberg, Maggie Scarf, James Masterson, Helen Bruch, Alice Miller, Anna Freud, Salvador Minuchin, John Bowlby, Theodor Reik, Merle Fossum, Marilyn Mason, Gershen Kaufman, Janet Woititz, Stephen Glenn and other talented clinicians listed in my bibliography, for their expert clinical knowledge and teachings and for challenging my heart and thoughts.

Peter Vegso and the staff of Health Communications, for providing long hours, talent and creativity in the publishing of *Children of Trauma.*

Lu Ann Jarvie and Gary Seidler for their consistent professional support, warmth and caring.

My clients, consultees and the participants in my seminars and workshops, without whose personal knowledge and sharing this book would never have been possible.

A Special Acknowledgment to the memory of Linda Zeigen and a heartfelt thank you to her husband, David, and children Josh and Kailin, for the opportunity of knowing a truly loving, caring and healthy family. I am grateful for your friendship.

DEDICATION

To Dr. Rudolph Moz . . .
   my husband and partner who has consistently
   provided loving support to me and my work and
   who has strengthened my path of clinical understanding.

To Alex E. Ward . . .
   my loving brother who provided the warmth of a
   "home" for me.

To Anna Latimer, Jo Ann Kauffman and Harold and Joy
   Belmont . . .
   without whose spiritual strength and guidance
   during rocky spots on the road, this book would
   never have been completed.

To the Families and Individuals With Whom I Have
   Worked . . .
   who have consistently taught me admiration and
   respect for the strength and beauty of the inner
   child.

TO MY CHILDREN

The following is dedicated to my sons: Shawn, Jason, Damien and Forrest Middelton, in heartfelt thanks for their loving support of my work and for sharing their unique perceptions of their world with me. I would also like to thank my step-daughter, Melinda Moz, for her support and for sharing of herself and for allowing me to be a part of her world.

My Eight New Eyes

by Jane Middelton-Moz

from *Juggler In A Mirror*

i never thought i would give birth
to four children
so i planned a career
and mourned the loss of motherhood
burying it away beneath books and tests
then they were all born
four sons in five years

i didn't have time
to plan how to raise them
so we raised each other
i taught them structure and discipline
and loved each for his unique self
shawn showed me the pain on the face
of the crippled circus clown
jason taught me the poetry
of the sun   the moon   and crackers
damien taught me to believe
in things i could not see
forrest taught me to make funny noises
and to find frogs in the muddiest swamp
all taught me of my humanness
and my stubbornness
i taught them how to walk and
pointed them in many directions
they in return brought back to me
eight new eyes to see the world

AN EXPLANATION

The individuals mentioned in the case examples are composites of many children of trauma who I have seen in my 22 years of clinical practice. The experiences of children of trauma are frequently similar. Any similarity of examples to specific individuals is only a result of these typical characteristics.

CONTENTS

Of Clouds And Seeded Dandelions

By Jane Middelton-Moz

from *Juggler in a Mirror*

A summer's day
When I was five
My mom was drunk
My bird had died
I went to church
To find in it
The Man called God to help a bit
He wasn't home

I walked to church
Across the road
Where a Man called Christ lived
I was told
He'd forgive my sins
Mother's too if she'd come in
The door was locked

A stone man stood beside the door
His eyes were tired
His back was sore
Holes were in His hands and feet
He could not touch me
Could not speak
The sign below said
No church will meet 'til Sunday

Now I watch the clouds drift by
The sun greets me in the sky
Shadows of the life I've lived
Present in these now
I can't enter doors that lock at night

Or worship a picture of one man's plight
Or the cross that stands on mother's grave

He wasn't home
She wasn't saved

I watched four dandelion seeds float by
Vessels drifting in the sky
Seeds of God can land in sand
Buddha, Moses, Christ and Man
Parched without the touch of life
Only stones that cannot speak

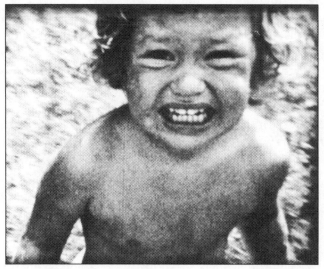

S.A. Harris

FOREWORD

This book is a long-awaited addition to the fine work Jane Middelton-Moz did in *After The Tears*, the book we wrote together two years ago. *Children Of Trauma* expands the scope of that work to include additional adult survivors of childhood traumas, both acute and cumulative. She focuses not only on the multigenerational numbing effects of substance abuse, neglect, sibling loss, sexual abuse, emotional abuse and parental loss, but also on the thousand little deaths suffered daily by children who are singled out for differences, whether because of ethnicity, poverty, religion, immigration or disability.

One cannot fail to appreciate the depth of empathy and sensitivity that Jane brings to this subject matter. She invites adult survivors to see themselves compassionately through a window to the child's pain and to view symptoms, such as panic attacks and dysfunctional relationships, as the child's attempt at mastery, rather than pathology.

Many current self-help books are cast in the victim/ villain mode and tend to deepen the already existing schism between these adult children, the larger culture and their families, particularly their parents. Jane avoids this pitfall by viewing individuals within the larger context. She creates a bridge by means of which healing becomes hopefully possible between adult survivors and their families of origin, whether living or dead. Jane recognizes that no matter how difficult a youngster's life circumstances were or no matter how inadequate a person's parenting might have been, the individual, at some level, both loves and needs to honor her or his parents and those who came before. Her goal is to foster not only healing at the individual level but also at the family system and cultural levels.

Jane's work reflects the depth of her clinical experience and her realistic view of the healing process in an arena sometimes characterized by limited clinical experience and an abundance of hyperbole. This is an excellent book, not to be missed.

Lorie Dwinell, MSW, ACSW

S. A. Harris

O N E

The Discarded Self, An Overview Of Children Of Trauma

Later In 1984

by Brook

this safe place i call
home of my mother:
what does it offer?
calamity was its fuel for heat.
sorrow fed our mouths for dinner.
and you, mother, i fear you still.

this place i call
home of my mother:
i say i no longer live here

1

but i find pieces of my heart
in each room.
must i claim them?
they are half eaten, half rotten.
i walk through the rooms.
step by step. piece by piece.
i place the pieces in a sack.
and you, mother, i fear you still.

this safe place i called
home of my mother:
i have my own home.
you have your sorrows. i have my pieces.
and you, mother, i fear you less.

Sandy

Standing still in the same spot for the past five minutes, the little girl remained perfectly erect. Her small-boned hands were clutched behind her. Her tiny leotard-covered legs were crossed at the ankles and held tightly together. The pressed white pinafore was without a wrinkle.

She spoke a little louder, "Mommy please, I need to go to the bathroom." Four, perhaps five years old, the little girl appeared much older. As she stood near her engrossed parents in Chicago's O'Hare airport, Sandy was too patient, too sedate for a normal child of her age.

Fighting in strained intense tones, her parents seemed oblivious to the child's persistent yet patient requests. Another few minutes passed. Slowly she reached up and touched her mother's arm. "Mommy, please!" The mother grabbed the little girl by her shoulders, "Well go then. Sandy, will you grow up? Can't you see I'm busy talking to your father? Go!"

While her parents resumed muffled retaliations above the noise of the airport hub-bub, Sandy backed away. Pulling herself even more erect, she started walking hesitantly down the crowded hall. A curious marionette in a well-starched pinafore, Sandy paused now and again. Trying her best to look grown up, she mostly appeared frightened, confused, alone.

Jimmy

Months and miles away, another child was playing quietly under the chairs of his mother's table in an airport cafeteria. Jimmy appeared to be about four. His very young mother painted and repainted her face, sipping cocktails with abrupt anxious movements. Every few minutes she would jump up and run to the door, nervously checking for the arrival of the plane for which she was so impatiently waiting.

Jimmy darted after her, "Wait, Mommy, wait!" She would turn, put one hand on her hip and point a threatening finger in his direction.

"Get back there! Do you want to ruin this relationship, too? Damn it, Jimmy, leave me alone!" Glaring at his mother, he retreated to the table and began taking sugar packets out of a bowl and tossing them one by one on the floor. For this behavior, Jimmy would get soundly shaken, slapped on the backside and banished to his stainless steel shelter. "Get back under there, you brat. You're just like your drunken old man! Stay out of the way!"

During one such interaction, the mother pushed her drink at him, trying to be careful that no one witnessed the offering. He drank some and made a face. She force-fed him some more, "Look at you, you like it, don't you? You're going to be a drunk just like that no good dad of yours!"

Dragging him out from under the table, his mom combed his hair with abrupt rough motions. Finished with his grooming, she stared at Jimmy with blank harshness and shoved him back under the table prison. He gazed up at his mom while she retouched her lipstick one more time.

Danny

In another place and time four-year-old Danny stood, eyes opened wide, marvelled by the abundance of a

department store toy section. The Yupik Eskimo child
was running his hand gently across the face of a blond,
white-skinned doll. His parents stood close by, silent,
stoic, glancing at him frequently, nervously. Their eyes
seemed to suggest, perhaps urge Danny to remember
that gentle touches were enough.

Across the aisle from Danny, a little white boy sat
cross-legged on the floor. Zooming a truck in circles
around himself, the boy filled the air with imitations of
diesel engines and airhorns.

After a time, the little boy's father, obviously frustrated from looking for his child, appeared at the end of
the aisle, "Damn it, son!" he yelled, "Get up off that
floor; you look like a drunk, squattin' Indian!"

Danny's parents looked away immediately. Their eyes
fell to the floor as they moved slowly toward their boy.
There was a sense of urgency in still downcast glances.
With hushed briskness, Danny's parents whisked him
out of the store. Not a word was spoken.

Cumulative Trauma

Sandy, Jimmy and Danny are children of trauma.
Throughout their developmental years they faced
"cumulative traumas" such as those described above.
(Kahn, 1963). They might never remember what really
happened, yet the buried feelings and emotional reactions
to these experiences may direct the course of their lives.
As adults these individuals may suffer from panic attacks,
bulimia, chronic depression, antisocial behavior, compulsive behavioral problems and addictions. The therapeutic
map and other necessary support required to work
through, resolve and master the traumas may never be
offered. They might not regain the discarded self that
was lost in a childhood over which they had no control.

Adult children of trauma often become locked in
unhealthy and addictive relationships. These patterns
reflect repeated survival attempts to master old pain.
They may choose not to have children, fearing they

would be unhealthy parents. If they do have offspring, these parents may not bond to their children or may become overenmeshed, overprotective or permissive. They may attempt to reparent themselves (through their children) in order to heal their own wounds.

Some children of trauma may eventually become leaders of corporations, doctors, psychologists, artists or poets. The pain and sensitivity of past experiences may help them create gifts to the world, yet many will treat themselves with disdain and neglect through workaholism, extreme perfectionism or chronic illness.

Better choices are possible. As adults these children can learn that they are survivors of trauma and look at themselves with feelings of respect for that survival. They can learn to believe in themselves enough to risk a long journey back through the pain. This process will allow them to reclaim their discarded self and free them to live, bond and break the generational cycle of pain. Sandy, Jimmy and Danny may risk allowing themselves to feel the initial pain of being welcomed to the planet earth, a welcoming that children of trauma may never have experienced.

Sandy, before the age of five, is already learning that it is not all right to have needs and feelings. She is an "unwelcomed visitor" who must take care of herself, control her needs and stay out of the way. In order to be accepted (allowed to stay), she must prematurely function like an adult. She is learning to focus on the needs of those around her and obliterate her most important developmental task: identity formation.

At the airport she was eventually taken to the bathroom by a well-meaning adult who was afraid for her safety. Sandy may have learned through this experience that strangers are more trustworthy than those responsible for her care. This lesson could have frightening implications for her if she continues to suffer the neglect experienced on this particular day.

Jimmy, on the other hand, is learning that he is more powerful than life. This lesson creates a tremendous lack of security and a need to act out more, seeking the outside controls which make him feel safe. He is learning that he can externalize his mother's anxiety and depression. Jimmy is also learning the blueprint for his life. He is bad, causes nothing but trouble and is destined to become an alcoholic. He has already tasted the liquid which may later sedate inner feelings of terror, pain and loneliness.

Danny's lessons may lead to the internalization of cultural self-hate. He is hearing that there is something wrong with him because of the color of his skin and the ways of his culture. The dolls he loves are not like him in color or features. Powerful figures on the family television set or officials in the school system are also different from him. He is already hearing a statistic which he may come to believe, that Indians are alcoholics (and doomed to die at earlier ages).

If his parents remain speechless about their own past pain and internalized shame, Danny will learn to hide his feelings to protect them from further distress. Ethnically or racially different childen are subject to a sense of shame that can turn into self-hate and intense isolation. If the parents have adapted to their own shame through learned helplessness, the child's world becomes divided. Ensuing conflicts in loyalties create an outside and inside reality that deeply injures a sense of self.

When we look at Sandy and Jimmy, we do not see behavior typical of happy-go-lucky, four-year-old children who have in only two years' time become comfortable with learning the "I." Nor do they within that knowledge begin really exploring their new world of self, asking hundreds of curious questions, showing expansiveness, energy and experimenting with language, cause and effect, imagination and tall tales.

Normal four-year-olds are busy learning to sort out the real from make-believe, questioning for the first time, "Where did I come from?" and "What happens when I die?" We see the curious child between four and five involving a parent for the first time in serious discussions of life. In both Sandy and Jimmy, however, we see children focused on parental behavior rather than their own developing language and curiosity. We do not see the shocked response of a traumatized child: frenzied, frozen, panicked and regressed. Instead, Sandy and Jimmy exhibit behaviors which indicate experience with trauma. They already show signs of massive defenses established through repeated traumas which make them less sensitive to emotional neglect and abuse. This can be likened to behavior adopted by soldiers experiencing war.

> "Soldiers can be hardened in training by the battle of experience; while certain physiological expressions of anxiety were considered normal in what was once called a soldier's baptism by fire, the seasoned soldier may take similar situations in stride."
>
> Waelder, 1967

No Trust, No Development

The energy a child expends to protect the self from frequent trauma, however, is energy that cannot be expended in normal child development. Basic trust in the security and continuity of the emotional and physical world are key to the development of a sense of positive identity and self-esteem.

Masterson (1985) talks about several elements that are present in a healthy real self. Among them are, "The ability to experience emotions deeply with liveliness, joy, vigor, excitement and spontaneity . . . the capacity to identify one's unique wishes and to use autonomous initiative and assertion to express them in reality . . . the capacity to limit, minimize and soothe painful emotions . . . the capacity to express the self fully in close relationships with minimal anxiety about abandonment or engulfment."

These capacities are sorely missing in adults who experienced regular unresolved traumas in their families. Or because of their parents' own traumatic childhoods, these children were not helped to resolve the traumas present in losses or in their ventures out into the world of school and community.

A child learns the trust and security of the world (through the unconditional love and nurturing of parents) in the initial weeks and months of life. This love extends beyond being fed and clothed. It is the warmth of the mother's body when being fed, the loving remarks and smiles of the parent when diapers are changed. Also involved is the early protective shield of the parents' holding the child. A sense of security develops also in the knowledge gained through repetition that although the parents may not always be right there every minute, they will return. In later months and years, while the child is building a sense of self, the parent's acknowledgment, praise, confidence, support, encouragement and comforting will be internalized by the child. This helps the child develop her or his own ability to express confidence in self, to self-praise for accomplishments, to self-encourage when confused and to self-soothe when disappointed. The parent's consistency and limits will be internalized as the child's self-discipline and self-control. The parent's positive attention to, and encouragement for the unique person the child is becoming, is positively internalized in the creation of the child's own sense of self and heightened self-esteem.

Children Of Trauma Of Children Of Trauma

Children of trauma are most frequently parented by individuals who experienced trauma that was never resolved. A child's first steps, when met with encouragement, cause the child to make greater steps forward. Children who experience disdain and judgment will be critical of themselves. If the parent shows anxiety and fear, the child will be unsure and tenuous or will take inordinate risks as a defense against fear. If the child's needs are rejected (as in the case of Sandy), the child will learn to show disdain for her own needs. This child leaps into expected responsibility of the pseudo-adult world with little or no foundation in reality. Typecast into a role and unable to live outside the world of the theater, this child excels at memorizing lines and remains dependent on the cues of various "directors."

Some children, like Jimmy, learn that normal childlike existence is a threat to the security of others. They learn that normal emotions are like weapons that can actually endanger the foundations of their parents' lives. With this internalized sense of self, they are equipped only to live out their identities as "bad apples," to become the alcoholic or "slut" their mother sees in them, abuse themselves for the contempt the parent shows or to turn the parent's anger on themselves, being afraid that to express it would create danger to others and to their sense of security. They may keep testing their environment to finally secure punishment for overpowering "crimes," committed before the age of five.

Children live out what they see reflected in their parents' eyes or in the eyes of others in their community. If what is reflected is the disdain and unacceptability of their developing self, that self will be discarded in order to meet the image in the reflective mirror of their world. The wall of internal defenses keeps their true self in check, a wall created by stimuli too great for an unprepared ego to endure. Children of trauma live in environments that stimulate emotions and simultaneously block their release. When the defensive wall is relaxed, as is the case of a soldier with no more wars, a workaholic without a job or a caretaker without someone to care for, what is seen is the original panic of the frightened child.

In her book, *The Ego and the Mechanism of Defense:* Vol. II, (1966), Anna Freud writes:

> "That the ego's defensive system acts as a protection against traumatization becomes evident whenever an individual is prevented from using a habitual defense in a situation that represents a specific danger for him. This

can be seen most clearly in cases of denial or of phobic avoidance . . . The phobic individual, who is forced to meet the object of her/his anxiety instead of avoiding it, is thereby forced undefended into a traumatic situation and breaks down in panic; so does the individual who has warded off a painful reality fact by denial (impending blindness, cancer, threatening loss of a loved one) and is forced to take cognizance of it against her/his own intentions."

The Trauma Of Minorities

The trauma faced by Danny is of a much subtler type, but the accumulation of such incidents over time can be equally as devastating to a child's self-concept. The trauma in this case is the continual erosion of self-esteem faced by ethnic and cultural minorities in a world where they are seen as lesser than others. The belief may develop early in these children's lives that their families lack power in the majority culture. Cultural and ethnic self-hate leads to a sense, deep in the core of the self, that "there is nothing I can do to make up for the lacking in myself and the awareness that I am deeply and profoundly unlovable."

This shame is frequently multigenerational. The child not only receives continual cues of his lack of power and lovability from the real world outside the family but may also feel it deeply from his parents whenever they have contact with the broader community. Although the child may pick up subtle cues from toys, books and television, he becomes most acutely aware of these differences when leaving the safety of home and entering school. He may be taunted, teased or merely recognize that the family left in the morning is very different than people encountered in the larger world.

As noted by child development expert Erik Erikson in *Childhood and Society*, 1950:

> "For a child of immigrant parents there is often acute conflict between the desire to look up to his parents and

the shame he feels for the exposure of their different ways and their uncertainty and unseemliness in a strange land. Estranged from both cultures he may manifest his own insecurity about where he belongs by over-zealousness in taking on the ways of the school and the neighborhood alien to his elders, and by impatience with their foreignness and slowness of adaption."

The exposure itself would not be as devastating to the child's developing sense of self if it were possible to discuss and explore feelings regarding early wounds with parents. Frequently, however, as may or may not be the case with Danny, the child picks up cues from the parents that they are themselves in pain and perhaps hurting and suffering more than he can ever presume to suffer. This feeling leads to the child's assuming a protective role reversal and a sense that nothing will ever make a difference. In many cases the child actually becomes a pseudo-adult ambassador for the parents to the strange and hostile world felt to exist outside the home. If a child feels that the parents suffer from irresolvable wounds to their own self-esteem, the child may also develop survival guilt. This guilt is likely to inhibit the child from experiencing a sense of success or joy beyond that of the parents. In contrast, some children tend to "identify with the aggressor" and develop a loathing for those like themselves as a defense against their own sense of powerlessness and self-loathing.

Self-Hatred

The deeply felt experience of self-hate is not limited to cultural or ethnic minority children. This process takes place for any child that feels the powerlessness of his differences in a broader world that cannot be expressed or validated at home.

A young child, for instance, with a perceptual handicap such as dyslexia, may feel the pressure from a school that does not understand the handicap. The child may be considered lazy, unmotivated or just one more behavior problem by teachers. Unaware or uninformed parents may see the child's behavior in the same light, not understanding the perceptual problem over which the child has no control. Without competent perceptual screening and testing, the child and parents may never understand why and how she is different. Instead, the child internalizes the beliefs of the adults and peers and feels that she is just "lazy" and "bad." This frequently leads to more behavioral problems, lack of motivation and severe depression. This sense of self-loathing can also be passed down the family tree and across generations.

Paula

Paula was aware from an early age that her father was different from other parents. Whenever they were out in public, he would become painfully shy and would sit far in the back at any public gathering. He was frequently depressed at home or would become enraged with her or her mother with little provocation, slamming doors and yelling, "You two feel better than everyone else. Well, I have news for you, I'm just as good as you are!"

Paula became very protective of her father and would feel disdain for those she felt were hurting him. When she was five, she realized that he could not read and quite innocently expressed this fact to her peers in the neighborhood. She was punished for this transgression by her mother, told that she had hurt her father deeply and was ordered to never again let anyone know her father could not read.

Paula became extremely compulsive about her own schoolwork and felt ashamed when she got less than an A. She studied constantly, never entering into the more social world of school and play. Her first love was a boy who she met in her junior year at college. He was an intellectual, a "bookworm" like herself, and their time together was spent sipping cokes after studying in the library. Their relationship broke up when he received a higher grade than she did on a final exam.

"I never want to see you again," she screamed. "You have always felt you were better than me; now you have your proof."

Paula's father delighted in her school successes, and he even began showing a sense of pride (that had always been lacking) whenever she brought home an honor. He would never, however, accompany her mother to her graduation ceremonies. Paula would become even more determined to try harder in school so that he would come when she received the next degree.

I saw Paula shortly after she had received her Doctor of Education degree. She had been hired as an assistant professor at a prestigious college in the East but had to leave the job because of severe panic attacks she experienced whenever she was required to stand up in front of her classroom.

Unresolved Trauma

All children experience traumatic events of one kind or another before reaching the age of 18. This fact is central in our treatment of children and adults who have experienced the effects of unresolved traumas in their lives. It is a fact we must also understand in order to appreciate and recognize healthy family interactions. Parents and extended family members cannot fully protect their children from traumatic events. They can, however, protect them from the damaging effects of unresolved trauma on the child's developing self-esteem.

For example, some children raised in alcoholic families do not show the typically damaging effects on self-esteem. If at least one adult family member was not in denial, the child's experience of trauma can be validated and her emotional reactions can be expressed. These two factors are essential if the child is to be assisted in mastering the traumatic events.

Children of trauma are individuals who were raised in families where denial is the primary defense used to cope with emotional pain. A child's sense of self is damaged less from the actual experience of the trauma than it is by the reactions of the significant adults in the child's life.

Sandler (1967) has observed that,

> "There is strong evidence that many children recover from truly traumatic experiences with little or no residual damage to their personalities. The degree of environmental support that the child receives is important here. What would seem to be crucial in deciding the outcome of a traumatic experience is not so much the experience itself, as the post-traumatic state of ego strain that it engenders in the child's adaption to that state."

Many survivors of sexual abuse, for instance, have shared that the failure to be believed when reporting abuse to an adult support person was far more devastating than the abuse itself. Likewise, children who have experienced the loss of a sibling in their childhood and had their feelings ignored because "they were only kids" show a devastated sense of identity. Many felt that they not only lost their brother or sister but also their parents because Mom and Dad failed to acknowledge the loss or grieve themselves. In some families the deceased sibling is never talked about again. Often failure to process the grief of a child's death results in divorce or emotional withdrawal of the parents from each other and their remaining children.

Many of the adults I have treated who lost siblings early in their childhood experience numerous problems: poor ability to connect with others, extreme dissociation, constant suicidal ideation and intense survival guilt. In some cases, because of their age at the time they experienced sibling death, or because of early rivalry and normal ambivalence, they have unconsciously believed that they killed the child. For others, the perceived lack of parental concern over the death resulted in the remaining child's internalized belief that the parents actually killed the brother or sister.

Many individuals have suffered extreme survival

guilt, never allowing themselves to truly experience life past the time of their sibling's death. These adults unconsciously believe that they should have died instead. They also feel that if they let their lives go on and detach from the constant memory of the dead sibling, no one will have cared. The parents' seeming lack of concern for the dead child is proof that the child never mattered to anyone and neither do they. Clinging to the dead child is the only way some children can validate their right to exist.

The four components necessary for the resolution of any trauma are: validation of the event, a supportive adult, validation of emotions and time. (Middelton-Moz and Dwinell, 1987).

In families where communication is open and healthy, where parents are not suffering from unresolved trauma and grief, validation, support, time and modeling are present.

For instance, if Danny's parents can talk to him after leaving the department store, model feelings for him, allow him expression and support, talk openly about the issues of prejudice and offer him skills to deal with the world outside his home, rather than deny their feelings and the prejudices that exist in others, he will not suffer injury to his self-esteem. It will be through their own denial, unresolved pain and inability to be emotionally present for him that his growing identity will be affected.

Connie

Connie is a very energetic five-year-old. Her drawings reflect a great deal of creativity and spontaneity. Occasionally, during shopping trips or while walking in the park with her dad, she will say, "Boy, Daddy, I really miss Mommy sometimes. I wish she were here with us." Rather than ignoring the subject or feeling the child's statement is an attack on his ability as an emotional caretaker, he stops and puts his arm around her.

"I know, it must hurt a lot sometimes. I miss Mommy, too. She used to come here with us. Are your remembering those times?" Connie's eyes fill with tears; her daddy's do also. They hug for a minute; then Connie grabs her dad's hand and they continue walking.

A little over a year ago Connie's mother died. She was hit by a car as she and her husband were walking back to their car after a late night out at a restaurant. Jim, Connie's dad, went immediately into shock. Even in his numb state, however, his first concern was his children. He called a friend for support and discussed how to tell them. The next morning after the children were awake, he gathered them together and told them directly and honestly that their mother had died the night before. Jim had his brother there as a support for himself. They all cried together frequently during the next few days.

Jim involved his children in the funeral arrangements. They took part fully in the grieving process. Jim sought out counseling and emotional support to deal with his feelings of loss and the traumatic event that caused his wife's death. He dealt with his rage at the driver who had killed her, as well as his own guilt. He asked himself over and over, what could he have done to prevent her death? He struggled endlessly with his own sense of helplessness. While working through his own grief, however, he remained as emotionally and physically available for his children as he could. He dealt with Connie's early night terror and her recurrent fear every time he would leave the house. He talked about his own loss and processed theirs with them.

About eight months after the death, Connie woke up in the middle of the night; she was crying and awakened her dad, "Daddy, I wish I could say happy birthday to Mommy. I wish Mommy were here. I miss her." After they had talked for a long time, they agreed to talk about it as a family the next day. Connie went back to sleep.

On his wife's birthday Jim and his children had a picnic in the backyard. They bought a huge bouquet of helium filled balloons and tied notes to them that said, "Happy birthday, Mommy." After they had eaten, they let the balloons go. The bright colors of the balloons stood out against the summer sky as they floated upwards and beyond while the children cried and sang "Happy Birthday."

For Connie and her brother the devastating effects of trauma on their personality development will not be present. Connie will not experience panic attacks at night whenever a loved one leaves the house nor compulsively overprotect her own children or need to emotionally detach from them. She will not have to leave relationships before she gets left or work her grief out in other relationships. Children who suffer unresolved trauma frequently act out in their adult lives the traumas they could not master in childhood fantasy and play. Because there was validation of her mother's death, validation of her feelings, her dad's modeling of appro-appropriate grief, someone there for her and time, Connie will have mastered the trauma.

We often fail to understand that people who behave outside the norm ultimately make sense. We may fail to see a person in the full context of her or his life. We may not ask questions, listen to what is said and not said. We may focus only on the panic attacks or compulsive behavior. We frequently see ourselves or others as an alcoholic, an overeater, a bulimic or an adult child of alcoholic parents. In this way we fail to see or hear that the many symptoms of trauma are truly attempts at mastery, self-protection and survival. Human beings are more than their behaviors.

A child may have grown up in an alcoholic family, have been sexually or physically abused, suffered the effects of a community or school where they were isolated and shamed, experienced the loss of a sibling or parent, watched Dad struggle with multiple sclerosis, lived in a country devastated by war or felt the humilia-tion of poverty. Individuals may have suffered some or all of these traumas and more, yet feel ashamed at their lack of perfection. They may never talk because no one has asked the questions or shown that they wanted to listen.

I have never worked with an individual who has been exactly like another. When we categorize, we dehumanize, even with the best of intentions. When we see others through our own experiences, rather than paying attention to what they see through theirs, we miss understanding the unique pain of the child inside them. As a result we will lack the full appreciation of the child's continual striving toward mastery, security and health.

Berkus said it best in his book, *To Heal Again*.

> "The quiet 'little deaths' of everyday existence are mourned as much as those of resounding magnitude, for grief makes no comparisons nor judgments and has no understanding of degree."

S. A. Harris

T W O

Where I Stop And You Begin: Developing Emotional Boundaries

Childhood Lost

by Brook

in a moment
from sleep
the flower
one petal at a time
perched in no privacy
declined from its flowerhood
left its stem
abandoned its smell
questioned its right to life
and brilliantly fell

miming its way
to the damp earth
to become
something else

Kate

Kate sat quietly, constantly smiling as she kept her hands carefully clasped together in her lap. Dressed in subtle tones, her methodically applied makeup barely noticeable, she seemed to want to be invisible. Always answering questions pleasantly, she never offered more than was requested.

She had come to therapy because she felt her life had become "meaningless." She suffered from continual headaches and other physical symptoms of stress. Kate had a good job and worked hard but had never received a promotion. She was too shy and rarely socialized with anyone at work. She had not been in a relationship in five years and had little understanding of why the last one had ended. Kate said she felt trapped in that relationship for two years but had waited for the man to end it because "You didn't want to hurt him." It had been her first love, but the relationship was a mystery to her.

Never quite sure how she felt, Kate referred to herself as if she were someone else, rarely using "I."

Middelton-Moz: How was your weekend at home, Kate?

Kate: About the same. You know when a person's there, she doesn't know what to do. Mom always does everything and Dad just complains. It's tense but you just keep going home every weekend. It's just the same; nothing ever changes.

Middelton-Moz: How would you like it to be different?

Kate: Well, you know, you'd like to feel comfortable with your family but you don't know how to make that happen.

Middelton-Moz: Kate, I have noticed that you rarely use the word "I" when referring to yourself.

Kate: My God, you just don't know you're doing that. *(There was a brief silence, then Kate began to laugh.)* I did it again. You're right, "I" don't.

Kate knew very little about her family. She had two younger sisters close to her in age. She remembered that as young children, they had all been dressed alike, were given the same things and the same privileges. They never fought because "you just didn't do that." Conflict made her father angry and when he was upset, everyone was upset. Her mother was always moving, "at least when Dad was home." She remembered few times with her sisters even though "the girls" all shared the same room. Kate did remember times she spent alone but not time spent alone with either parent. She described her mother as "always nervous" and her dad coming home from work "angry."

"When he was home, we just stayed out of the way." She remembered one occasion (when she was about seven, her sisters six and five), being lined up in a grocery store by their dad and severely scolded in front of people for fighting with each other. She recalled the sense of shame she felt and said she wished she could have disappeared. When she and her sisters would fight, her mom would cry and get sick to her stomach. Kate would feel extremely guilty whenever this happened.

Kate's parents' families lived within miles of them when Kate was young. Yet the only contact they had was once a year on New Year's Day. The gatherings were tense and Kate's mother remained busy. Her father rarely spoke or moved from his chair. When Kate was asked to complete a family map, she was surprised to realize that she had never heard her parents speak about their family histories. Kate felt awkward talking with them about "personal things" and chose instead to request the information from her father's only sister. She was amazed by what she learned. Her parents had been high school sweethearts who had come from very different economic backgrounds. They had been rejected by both families when they announced marriage plans.

Kate's father came from an extremely poor family. His parents had immigrated from Poland when they were adolescents. After his mother had died in childbirth, his father had stayed away from home working most of the time. The children had been left at home to fend for themselves.

Her mother had come from an upper-class family, and Kate had thought her to be an only child. Kate was surprised to learn that her mother had an older sister who had died tragically in a fire.

Both of her parents suffered traumatic childhoods. Their extremely different cultural and economic backgrounds had caused enormous stress in their marriage. Both families were bound in secrets, suffered unresolved pain and were ladened with shame. Upon seeing the generational legacies spelled out on the genogram (family map) before her, Kate exclaimed, "No wonder everything has always been so tense. I thought my parents' unhappiness began with us kids."

Kate showed characteristics of a child raised by parents suffering from unresolved trauma. Because of their own pain, her parents had been incapable of bonding to their children. Kate, therefore, was unable to form attachments. She had extremely low self-esteem, saw herself as unlovable and had difficulty maintaining her own emotional boundaries. To protect herself from further pain and rejection, she had lived her life in isolation, attempting to remain "invisible." She was unable to trust others because she was unsure of her ability to trust herself. She had continued in an unhappy relationship. It was safer to focus on her partner's needs, rather than to begin the process of recovering her discarded self.

Kate had difficulty identifying feelings. When she did feel anger, she was terrified by it, feeling her emotion was powerful enough to injure those around her.

Alice Miller (1981) states that a serious consequence of the child's needing to adapt to the parents' needs, rather than vice versa, is "the impossibility of consciously experiencing certain feelings of his own (such as jealousy, envy, anger, loneliness, impotence, anxiety) either in childhood or later in adulthood."

Like many children of trauma, Kate never developed emotional boundaries. She was a child who did not receive a welcoming of self from her family. She learned that she was responsible, required to please and needed to stay out of the way before she was developmentally aware that she was a separate person. Her unique self was not valued or accepted. She never learned that she was an individual and consequently could not, as an adult, separate herself emotionally from the needs of others around her. She had never learned "I am."

Identity Development

To understand the development of identity and the resulting development of emotional and physical boundaries, it is helpful to use the stages of identity constructed by Erikson (1950). His model describes eight stages of identity development:

1. Basic Trust versus Mistrust
2. Autonomy versus Shame and Doubt
3. Initiative versus Guilt
4. Industry versus Inferiority
5. Identity versus Role Confusion
6. Intimacy versus Isolation
7. Generativity versus Stagnation
8. Ego Integrity versus Despair

In the process of learning the lessons of these consecutive stages, an individual grows from total dependence (a self without boundaries) to becoming an individual separate from one's parents. The child moves from "that I am" to "who I am." Children who grow up in a healthy family and community environment learn boundaries.

They learn to appreciate themselves as unique individuals and value themselves in the broader world outside the safety of family. From a place of confidence in self, they are able first to develop true intimacy with another, then move to parenting their own children. In order for an individual to pass in a healthy way through each stage of identity formation, the one before must be successfully completed.

In families where parents have not been able to develop identity fully, it will be impossible for them to pass on developmental lessons to their children. A parent who has not learned that she is a uniquely valued self cannot see the beauty of her child's unique developing identity.

In families where unresolved trauma is an issue, children are forced to jump entire stages of development in order to survive. They move into adulthood without the necessary emotional, and sometimes physical, boundaries required to provide enough safety to continue on to new stages of development. Without a sense of trust, for example, it is risky for a child to develop true value in an autonomous self. Without learning that one is autonomous, it is impossible to develop intimacy with another.

Kate, for example, showed the inability to form a relationship in which she could risk conflict in order to feel intimacy. She had never learned to trust and therefore never developed a boundary between self and others. She could only feel safe when alone or when disappearing into the needs of others. Rather than learning that she was valuable as a person, Kate learned from her parents that self-worth was dependent on her earning their approval.

We Are One:
In Trusting You I Will Learn To Trust Me

At birth children are not able to perceive a difference between self and the primary parent. It is a stage of total dependence. If parents are without encumbrances from the past, they will aid their infants in learning trust. Children fully welcomed as individuals will be shown that their physical and emotional needs are of prime importance. Small children shown that they belong will learn that they have meaning and are prized. During this stage the parents temporarily give up their own needs for the needs of the infant. Parenting at this stage goes far beyond feeding and safety. It is the way in which the parent holds the child that teaches the infant that she or he is whole and beautiful. The loving look of admiration in the parent's eyes will become internalized as self-love and admiration. It is the comfort and soothing given that will become the child's ability to soothe and give comfort to self. The parent's consistency in care allows the infant to internalize the warm picture of that consistent parent and eventually develop trust. The infant learns the important lesson that even when alone, internally someone is always there.

> "The infant develops means for doing without constant care. This is accomplished through the accumulation of memories of care . . . confidence in the environment."
>
> Davis and Wallbridge, 1981

The infant who has trusted the environment by successfully placing personal needs in the hands of parents who are consistently there will incorporate that trust and safety inside himself. The child will also incorporate into his building sense of self the warmth and care of loving eyes.

In this first year of life the infant has learned to trust, first in the parent, then in self for periods of time alone. Erikson (1963) believed, furthermore, that it was in these earliest months of life that an individual learned to trust in something unseen outside the self that he would later incorporate as the capacity to experience spirituality.

Infants' experiences in this early stage will set the foundation for the development of trust in their environment, love and trust in self, capacity to believe and trust in things not always seen, the capacity to self-soothe and confidence in being alone. As easily as trust can be learned, however, so can mistrust.

Let us consider, for instance, the debilitating effects on development for an infant born during wartime where the emotional needs of the child cannot come first. Perhaps the parents, instead of living in a war zone, are preoccupied in a warring marriage or under the influence of mind-altering drugs or are themselves still children. The infant may be left unattended frequently and need to depend on an undeveloped self. The child may not have had the time to master confidence in even short periods of alone time. If the child is unfortuante enough to resemble a despised or feared person in the parent's life, what may then be reflected back to the child are eyes filled with disgust or fear instead of love. Maybe the infant's tears stimulate the unresolved dependency needs the parent fears in self. Perhaps the sound of the infant's crying, instead of signaling need, stimulates parental rage at the child's accusations of incompetence.

If the child is born handicapped in some way and becomes a threat to the parents' need for perfection, the message through the detached holding of this child may be that the self is not whole or acceptable. An infant, who is only physically cared for or who is merely fed and clothed but not responded to or interacted with, will experience the threat of self-annihilation rather than learning the beginnings of trust and self-confidence.

> "Within the context of ego-support, the environment acts upon the baby in a way that is within the baby's competence because it is predictable and because the mother has the baby in her mind as a person . . . when there is a lack of ego support or a lack of protection, the environment impinges upon the baby in such a way that the baby must react (for example, repeated change in technique, loud noises, head not supported, baby abandoned, etc.), the continuity of being is interrupted. When the baby cannot rest and recover within an environment that has once more become maximally adaptive, the thread of continuity cannot easily be

restored. An accumulation of traumatic impingements at the stage of absolute dependence can put at risk the stability of the individual."

Davis and Wallbridge, 1981

In the environment of unresolved trauma, mistrust is learned. The child learns self-contempt rather than self-soothing, fear of aloneness rather than competence, mistrust rather than trust and the development of a reactive self rather than the development of the unique and beautiful true self. Many adults, therefore, go through life either merely surviving in total isolation, terrified to trust in self or others, or move from relationship to relationship, terrified of being alone, feeling an inability to be secure when not enmeshed with another. These adults have never been able to internalize a loving, caring parent who was first with them, then inside them. They were not allowed to develop gradual competency in being alone. They were instead forced to leap into new developmental stages unequipped, without mastering the very elemental lesson of trust.

Mother

by Don Nelsson

We never sat down and really talked,
Not about ourselves, our feelings.
Now you are gone and "I" to follow.

There were glimpses you gave
To a boy too shy to probe further.
Now you are gone and "I" to follow.

A few times you talked of yourself
I was skeptical
You were used to stretching the truth,
Not maliciously, but to save others
From truth.

I still can't recognize the truth,
Always doubting.
Now you are gone and "I" to follow.

Our chance is done, there is no other.

Fred

Fred was the unwanted child of an adolescent mother. As an infant he was left unattended for long periods of time while his mother slept, reportedly exhausted from working nights. His mother's parents were "hyper-religious" and would not let her give the child up for adoption. This resulted in early months filled with neglect and inconsistency, with Fred's dependency needs ignored through her abandonment. He learned from his environment that he did not belong and that his needs were unimportant. Since he was not held and cuddled, soothed with gestures and words or treated with loving care, he could not internalize these feelings concerning himself. With such inconsistent parenting, Fred could not internalize someone being there and did not have the opportunity to slowly learn to soothe himself during brief periods of time alone. He learned mistrust of self and others. Fred's mother had been quite relieved when he was eventually taken from her custody.

Because of his new mother's need to overcome the trauma of her own unhappy beginnings through Fred's childhood (as an orphan she had been placed in one facility after another), Fred was forced to develop further denial of real self. When he would cry as a child or appear the least bit fearful, Fred's adoptive mother would become frustrated and angry, telling him that he was "letting his neglectful mother win over him." This increased the development of his already building false self, rather than allowing resolution of the pain of infant trauma in a safe new environment. Fred was not allowed to develop trust in himself but was forced instead to react to the world around him.

Fred was 47 when his fourth wife left him. He came into therapy for the first time the day after she moved out of the house. He had not been able to eat or sleep when alone. He felt constantly fearful and was extremely depressed and full of self-loathing. Fred told me that he had never lived by himself. He had gone from his adoptive parents' house to sharing an apartment with his "first love." From there he had moved in with his first wife. Then he got involved in an affair, that woman eventually becoming his second wife, and so on. He alternately blamed himself and his wife for the breakup. He hated his feelings of dependency and in each relationship had come to despise the woman for "making him dependent." He said that he was never able to stand up for himself against women who wanted to control him. He also said he had always had "someone waiting in the wings." This time he had not. He had been surprised by his wife's decision to leave the marriage for someone else. Within two weeks of our first meeting, Fred abruptly moved in with a woman from work, acknowledging that he thought the move was impulsive but was sure she was right for him. His anxiety immediately decreased.

Fred said that he had always been terrified to be alone. "I can't believe it's possible that I am still terrified. I'm a full grown adult man, not a wimp. I'm the head of my own business, for God's sake, but without a woman at home, I feel I can't survive. It should be mind over matter, right? Simple."

I Am: The Critical Lessons Of Autonomy

Jason and Theresa

A bright-eyed little boy in a navy blue and white sailor suit sat playing with the assortment of toys spread out before him on the floor. He grabbed on to his mother's leg and pulled himself to a standing position. His mother looked down from her magazine, ruffled his hair and continued reading. Holding on to her chair, he carefully made his way to the next, then the next, stopping at each one and glancing up at his mother. Every now and then, she would look at him and smile. Certain that she was aware of him and there for him, he would proceed carefully to the next chair. When he had reached the fourth chair, his mother gently said, "What a big boy you're getting to be. Come back to Mommy now, Jason."

Jason did not return, but did not go any further. He just started patting the chair in front of him. Then discovering a magazine on the next chair over, he reached for it, grabbed it and began shaking it around.

"What's that you have? It makes noise, doesn't it?"

Jason giggled, shaking the magazine. All of a sudden, he let out an excited cry as he spotted a large, shaggy, stuffed dog. The toy was lying in front of a quiet, sedate little girl who was sitting on the floor across the room. Pointing in her direction, Jason dropped the magazine.

"Doggy," his mother said, replying to his excited gesture.

The mother of the little girl looked at him, seemingly irritated, then glanced at her child. The little girl, still sitting quietly next to the big plush animal, spied Jason's discarded toys and pointed.

"No, Theresa!" her mother said firmly. "Sit still. Be good."

Theresa's mother watched her somber daughter for a minute, apparently assuring herself that her daughter had heard her instructions. She glanced toward Jason with a look of disgust, then went back to her magazine.

Jason, meanwhile, still stood with eyes opened wide, looking at the strange shaggy animal. Every now and again he would make an excited noise, point, then glance at his mother. She would smile and talk with him about the unfamiliar object of Jason's budding curiosity.

All of a sudden Jason took off across the floor. He wobbled back and forth with excited noises. He seemed proud of himself, as if he had just invented this strange locomotion. He stopped abruptly after several steps as if aware for the first time of what he was doing. He plopped to the ground with a start, his face still holding a shocked expression.

His mother watched, appearing to be as surprised by Jason's first steps as he was.

"Jason! What a big boy! You're walking!" His mother's face was simultaneously laughing and crying when she moved toward her stunned son. Jason was wildly gesturing at her, not sure whether to laugh or cry. His mother picked him up, held him close and praised him for his new accomplishment.

"Just wait until we get home. I wish Daddy could have been here. He'll be so proud."

After a few minutes of holding, Jason regained his composure and seemed to remember what all this was about in the first place. He pulled slightly away from his mother's arms and pointed again at the dog. His mother, aware of his wishes, walked up to Theresa and her mother, "Is it all right if Jason visits your friend?"

Theresa did not move, but her mother looked up with a forced smile. "I guess it's all right if he looks at Shaggy, but . . .," she appeared apologetic, "well, Theresa doesn't like other children playing with her things. She likes to keep them good."

Jason's mother walked over and picked up one of his toys. "Why don't we let Theresa play with Mr. Tipsy, while you pet her doggy?" She placed the brightly colored rolly clown in front of Theresa, then held Jason firmly in front of Shaggy, guiding his little hand in petting motions. "Now only pat him gently, Sweetheart. Theresa's mother doesn't want you to play with her things, but she will let you pet him."

Jason, with his newly acquired form of mobility, is beginning to learn that he is a separate person from his mother. In those initial tentative movements away, he is learning, "I am." His mother is allowing him some space from her to explore his world while still remaining supportive and protective. She is letting his developing interest in his world grow and expand within the context of her encouragement and support. She is also letting him know that she approves of both his venturing away as well as his need to return to her. He is beginning to learn choice and approval for the beginnings of independence rather than feeling unlovable for movements away. She is supporting his choices; therefore, he will learn confidence in them rather than shame and doubt.

Theresa, on the other hand, is not exploring or moving away. Instead, she appears almost frozen, captive to her mother's need for what she calls a "good child." Her mother's needs for compliance, cleanliness and adult-like behavior in a child of 13 to 15 months are keeping Theresa from exploring her new and appropriate sense of self. Instead of learning "I am," Theresa is learning "I am an extension of someone else." If this interaction between herself and her mother continues, she will learn to feel unlovable when not pleasing another and will have doubts regarding her own choices. Instead of learning to explore a new sense of self, Theresa is learning to restrict her movements.

A child develops a sense of self through contact with the world. If the child's attachment to that world is through a fearful parent, the child will learn to fear. If the parent's sense of self comes only through the behavior of the child, the child will have to be "good" or "special" for the parent to feel a sense of positive identity. The child's growth will be stifled by the parent's unresolved issues of self. A child cannot risk parental disapproval at this stage of development without risking the abandonment from her major attachment to the world. The child learns in unhealthy attachment that she is lovable only when meeting the needs of the parent. The child develops bond permanence to the parent rather than further development of self.

Consider, for instance, what might happen to Jason's sense of developing autonomy if his mother had experienced the death of a child before he had been born. Perhaps she had never grieved the loss of that child and Jason became a replacement for grief. Instead of being a uniquely developing little boy of 12 to 15 months, he would exist in the tragic shadow of a dead brother or sister. Perhaps his mother felt guilty over the sibling's death and became rigidly overprotective of Jason. When he began to explore the world around him in the waiting room, she might abruptly bring him back to her, not let him explore, hold him constantly or confine him to a playpen. Jason would soon learn that his growing interests in the world were "bad" or "unsafe" and that his growing need for autonomy was undesirable. His sense of curiosity in the touch and sounds of the magazine would result in checking out his mother's reaction, rather than exploring his own. His beginning explorations of interest, curiosity and autonomy would be replaced by doubts in his own movement and shame in self-exploration. He, like Theresa, would need to replace his sense of self with an image acceptable to the world around him.

Adults who achieve success but can never believe that they are successful, or individuals who are afraid to feel or react without checking the reaction of the world around them, were once children who were not allowed to experience the success of their own developing autonomy. They saw in the eyes of those around them distortions in early attempts at exploration. Those distortions were internalized as evidence of their own unlovability or as self-doubts in curiosity, exploration and autonomy.

When Theresa was first presented with the brightly colored clown by Jason's mother, she reached out with exploring hands and grabbed it cautiously. She let out a little shriek as Mr. Tipsy rolled from side to side. "Now, play quietly, Theresa," her mother said abruptly. "Be a good girl." Theresa drew her hands back and looked up into her mother's disapproving eyes. She then moved to her mother, hiding her eyes behind her mother's skirt.

> "Shame is early expressed in an impulse to bury one's face, or to sink, right then and there, into the ground. But this, I think, is essentially rage turned against the

self. He who is ashamed would like to force the world
not to look at him, not to notice his exposure. He would
like to destroy the eyes of the world. Instead, he must
wish for his own invisibility."

Erikson, 1963

The 12- to 15-month-old child begins to explore the
world on her or his own with new skills in movement.
At two years of age, the child further asserts "I am" in
language: "No!" and "I want." This may be seen as being
negative or rejecting the parent when in fact the child is
just more determined to become a person in her or his
own right. The child at this age may defiantly refuse to
be held and at the same time stubbornly refuse to give
up the treasured "blanky" that held her or him in
infancy. Treasured objects like the first teddy bear or
blankets provide a valuable security between the
warmth of a parent's lap and the need to establish bonds
with the new world of a separate reality. The blanket
may become torn, dirty, dragged everywhere, be
neglected and then retrieved, but must never be taken
away until the child willingly gives it up for new
developmental pursuits. It is the child's first milepost
between the world of "me" and "not me." It can be loved
and hated and still surive. (Davis and Wallbridge, 1981).

The child needs to learn from the relationship with
the parent the same lesson practiced with the blanket,
that the parent can be loved, needed, hated and still
survive. This is a lesson that the child will carry forth to
all intimate relationships established in the future, that
you can love and be loved, be angry and have others
angry at you and still survive. It is a lesson that allows
intimacy without loss of self.

"In terms of personal relationships, the change means
that the same live person can be loved and hated,
protected and attacked without magically changing in
quality, because that person is felt to exist in their own
right, as separate and permanent."

Davis and Wallbridge, 1981

If the parents' unresolved needs supersede the child's developmental tasks, the child will not be able to grow as a fully emotionally autonomous self. The crucial developing boundary between the "me" and "not me" (Winnicott, 1971) will suffer as a result. A parent's need for a clean and perfect environment or for a mature "adult child" may replace the child's need for the blanket. A parent who needs the child's continual adoration to support injured self-esteem, will not be able to tolerate the child's "no's" or anger. Instead of learning that love can exist simultaneously with anger and conflict, the child will repress her or his anger and expressions of self in order to maintain connectedness with another. The lesson that will be learned is that "others cannot survive my expression of self."

Children who have not learned that anger, conflict and love can exist simultaneously and that conflict can be resolved will become adults that hold their emotional selves hostage in intimate relationships.

Children in early stages of emotional boundary development need the supportive and caring limits of a parent. They need parents who will support and protect them in initial ventures into the new world of separate reality. The child needs to be able to express emotions, receive caring limits on the degree of expression and realize the parent can survive the expression in order to develop the "I am" without repression or need for excessive internal controls from an underdeveloped ego. The child learns from this first venturing of self with others the ability to be angry and repair those feelings with another. These experiences will later develop into the capacity for true empathy in relationships rather than repression of self.

Parents stuck in their own need for repair and approval have difficulty with supportive limits. They tend to either permissively reparent their own child or cannot allow the expression of their child's newly developing sense of self without viewing such expression as attack. The child's emotional developmental needs for the boundary "I am" can be held captive by unresolved traumas of parental pasts. Children of trauma may venture into future development without the protection of the space that exists between the "me" and "not me" and become indiscriminately fused to others in an attempt to merely survive.

The Growth Of Internalized Limits And Empathy Versus Debilitating Guilt

Koolaid Stand

by Nanci Presley-Holley

I opened a door
The one that sits on top of my head
The memories flooded in.

I remember standing in the car
    behind my mother's seat,
as she sobbed and cried in fear;
'cause she'd spent too much on groceries,
    and for that she'd get beat.
I patted her on her shoulder
To comfort as best I could.
But I was just three,
and she would have none of that.
That was the first day I had my Koolaid stand.
I tried to give her my pennies,
But she turned away and laughed out loud.

It wasn't the first time.
And it certainly wasn't the last.

Joey

Three-year-old Joey loved shopping trips to the store with his mom. The colors, smells and interesting shapes were nearly too much for his three-year-old self to endure. First he spied the huge cookies in the bakery showcase, "I want one! I want one!" His mother, concentrating on the bread for that night's dinner, appeared to ignore his pleas. Becoming louder, more adamant, Joey reached up and pulled on his mother's blouse, "I want cookie!" Directing her attention to her son, Joey's mother reached in her purse and retrieved a large, wholesome cookie. "I know you want those, sweetheart, but Mommy brought you a snack from home." Initially, Joey was reluctant to accept his mother's offering. After all, the cookies in the case had brightly colored M & M's. Soon, however, her patient coaxing succeeded and he accepted the replacement.

A short while later, another battle ensued. At the checkout counter Joey spied the colorful comics, "Supaman, Supaman. I want it!" His mother again reached into her overstuffed bag and produced his favorite book, "Look, Joey, *The Little Engine That Could.*"

"No! No! Supaman!" he screamed, reaching with such force that he almost fell out of the cart.

His mother gave him the replacement book which he immediately threw to the floor with great force. "I don't want it! Supaman!" He swung his little arms wildly and hit his mother's arm in the process. She picked him up out of the cart, "No, Joey, I can't let you have it and I won't let you hit." After a few minutes of intense pulling away, Joey collapsed in tears on his mother's shoulder. "I know you want it, sweetheart, but you can't have it." A few minutes later, Joey was placed back in the seat of the loaded grocery cart, having accepted the favored book his mother offered.

After paying for the groceries, Joey's mother spoke to the clerk, "You know, I wish you would speak to your manager for me. It's very hard on children to have these comics sitting right here at the check-out counter. I know you want to sell them, but perhaps they could be placed on display somewhere else in the store."

The woman understood perfectly and returned Joey's mother's smile. "I know just how you feel. I have children, too, but the fact is, they sell here. You'd be surprised at how many mothers and fathers give in to tantrums and buy them. I'll speak to the manager, though."

David

The words of the clerk were accurate. Minutes after Joey left the store with his mother, David and his mother approached the check-out counter. David's face was covered with chocolate and streaked with tears. His mother looked like she had barely survived a war. David started screaming, "I want! I want! I want Spidaman!"

"No, damn it," his mother yelled, "I bought you a cookie, that's it. You want everything you see."

"I want it now!" David screamed. "Now! NOW!"

"You're not getting it. Stop being a brat. I've had it with you!"

David started wildly swinging his arms, hitting his mother in the process. She picked him up out of the seat, hit him hard on the bottom a number of times and tossed him back in the cart seat. David began to wail. His mother, apparently feeling guilty for her loss of patience, then picked up the comic and handed it to him. "Okay, okay. I'll buy it for you."

David took the comic, sniffled for a few minutes, then reached for his mother, "Mommy, Mommy."

"No, I'm not talking to you the rest of the day. You're a bad boy. You got the comic, now leave me alone." She looked at the clerk who appeared accustomed to this scene, "I can't wait until he grows up, but he's got to learn right from wrong."

No one can argue with the statement that children need to learn right from wrong. David's mother, however, may well be teaching him lessons that she never intended to teach. In this instance, he is learning that if he protests strongly, he will get what he wants for a price. He is learning that his drives are stronger than his mother's limits; that fighting and being hit eventually pave the way to getting what he wants; that love is sacrificed in the getting. David is being shown immediate gratification for wishes on the one hand and guilt for getting needs met on the other. He may have to continue acting out to get limits and perhaps never learn self-control, or may put more controls on himself than his development can handle in order to gain his mother's affection.

Children are not born with a conscience (that voice inside that tells us right from wrong) or empathy (the ability to feel what other's might feel in a similar situation). Conscience and empathy do not grow automatically as our bodies do but develop through the lessons taught by the adults involved in the child's early life.

Most of us know of adults who appear to have no sense of right or wrong, who seem to have little empathy for others in their lives. We also know individuals who seem to have a rigid, non-empathic internal policeman who holds them responsible for everything, including the actions of others around them. There are some people who blame their behavior on others and those who believe someone is constantly watching or "out to get them." In addition, there are individuals who know right from wrong, take responsibility for their choices and feel empathy for others without taking responsibility for the moods and behaviors of others. All of these adults learned lessons regarding self-responsibility and care for self and others early in their development — such as David and Joey are in the process of learning at the grocery store.

The controls and limits given to children by parents during early stages of development will later become the consciences they will have as adults. It is a process that develops gradually from age two through adolescence. It is a patient exchange of teaching and learning. The firm yet kind and loving parental voice of Joey's mother will be the internalized, kind and firm limit that Joe will have on himself as an adult and eventually, perhaps, teach to his own child.

If a true conscience does not develop in a child until the fifth or sixth year, one might ask, "What of those

well-behaved two- or three-year-olds as we all know?"
What about compliant Theresa in the last section?

Theresa, as we saw in the previous section, has had to
forfeit her own developing self for survival. She has not
begun the process of separation, let alone the development of a conscience. She has instead developed a strict
uncompromising internal policeman who shows no
empathy or love for her. She had to invest the energy
normally given to development to repression of self
(emotions, desires and motivations). Theresa suffers
from prohibition of instincts rather than guidance of
them. She may become a child and later an adult who
continually suffers from nightmares, physical illness and
paralysis of feelings. She may never know the joys of a
truly intimate relationship or experience sexual pleasure.
She may be continually depressed or cling to those for
whom she feels the most anger. It is sometimes difficult
to understand that those children who show acting-out
behavior in school and those who are extremely "good"
both suffer from lack of true internal conscience
development. They both pay the price: one from the
need for external controls and one from rigid uncompromising internal controls. It is true that extremely
permissive parents (as well as overly strict parents)
produce children who do not adequately develop
empathy and conscience. In both cases children must
depend on external sources rather than gradually
developing their own internalized boundaries of right
and wrong.

Linda

Linda's mother was extremely strict. She fought
continually with her daughter, stating that she was
going to make her a "good" child. Linda's mother had
come from a strict repressive family. She had been the
"bad" child who had never pleased the parents in the way
her older sister had. She had finally made her mother
proud when she had given birth to Linda, the first
grandchild. It was as though by having a child, she had

finally lived up to family expectations. She had divorced her husband shortly after Linda's birth, and her parents had supported this action, saying that he was not good enough for her or her new daughter.

The fights between Linda and her mother began with toilet training. At two, Linda was afraid of the sounds of the "big toilet" but her mother and grandmother forced her to sit on it "like a big girl." After many weeks of fighting, Linda was not allowed to use diapers and was forced to "either go on the floor" and get spanked, or "use the toilet like a good big girl." Linda became so constipated that she was finally hospitalized. About that same time she started having nightmares every night and became terrified of taking her bath, which had in the past been an enjoyable activity.

By the time Linda was four she was being repeatedly locked in her room whenever she was angry. On some occasions, however, she would be invited by her mother to throw pillows at the wall and pretend it was her father. During this period, Linda developed severe stomach pains and began reporting nightmares of monsters with huge teeth that tried to "eat her up."

Linda's mother's parenting style reflects delayed trauma from her own early childhood years. She still wrestles with "good" and "bad" and Linda became involved with that unresolved struggle. We can also see in Linda's early nightmares and physical symptoms, extreme stress resulting from attempts at the development of premature self-control. The big-mouthed "giants" can be seen in light of her own repressed anger, the anger that is now "going to eat her up." It must also be extremely confusing for Linda to receive controls on her feelings and at the same time be guided by her mother's modeling to express that same previously censored rage at her father. Without intervention and depending on other models in her life, it would not be surprising to see Linda as an adult with severe panic attacks, chronic physical illnesses, bulimia, chronic depression or as an adult who cannot unify the split between "all good" or "all bad."

Just as the blanket, thumb or prized teddy bear becomes a transitional object between "Me" and "Not Me" (Winnicott, 1972), so do imaginary friends and nightmares often represent the transitions between the need for external controls and internalizing that control in the development of true conscience. It is not unusual to hear a three-year-old child blame all her unacceptable behavior on a newly invented imaginary friend. We can see with this new creation that the child is beginning to find the behavior unacceptable without the means to control it.

Nightmares and early childhood fears are indications that children are beginning to attempt to control behavior. If the nightmares or fears become excessive, however, it is frequently a sign that the adults in the child's life are expecting too much internal control at too young an age. It is often difficult for a parent to understand that even though the child is "bigger" in many ways, she is still not capable of internally controlling behavior. The development of that internal boundary takes patience, loving teaching and time. The child who seems so good too early is often a child who was prematurely forced to put controls on self and that control will affect future development. Parents who need to have their child behave in a particularly "good" way or, conversely, cannot set firm yet loving limits on misbehavior, are adults who have been rendered incapable of seeing the child as a child. This is often the result of the parents' own early unresolved traumas or current traumas in the family that affect their very survival — war, extreme poverty, difficulty in immigration, debilitating illness.

Selma Fraiberg (1959) presents the case of a little girl, age three, who enjoys the pleasure of squashing caterpillars on the sidewalk and gleefully examining the remains. That same child at age six becomes upset and sad at the thought of a dead insect, bird or animal. What has happened inside that little girl was not the automatic miracle of development, but rather the careful and patient teaching of parents that has now been internalized by the child as empathy, compassion and a developing conscience. If that same child, however, at age six showed an extreme response, losing herself when an animal or human was hurt or sad, or still enjoyed smashing caterpillars or intentionally hurting animals, we would have cause to be concerned about the adequate progression of developmental learning in this child's life.

Joey's mother, at the beginning of this section, shows understanding of his growing development. She has given forethought to the trip to the grocery store, having anticipated temptations from a small child's point of view, and came prepared with substitutions for his wants. These substitutions will not be necessary at age five when Joey has more ability for internal control. She is also capable of setting firm limits without telling Joey that his desires or emotions are "wrong." Being upset and angry is natural under the circumstances, hitting is not acceptable. The limits at this age are as important as the understanding.

It is important for the developing child to be able to keep imaginary friends without being allowed to hold "them" responsible for her behavior. The child who never takes that next step, to internalize that mischievous playmate, may be holding others accountable for her behavior as an adult. The little girl that is squashing the caterpillar needs to receive guidance from her adult figures rather than punishment for her young impulses. A child, who at age two is angry at a new baby sister, needs to be taught that her anger is normal, but hitting is not allowed. Before the age when the child can be taught to verbalize feelings, it may be appropriate to offer an inflatable clown to punch (Fraiberg, 1959). After the child reaches an age when she can be taught to verbalize, however, offering such a substitution for an outlet of physical aggression would be inappropriate guidance. Encouraging the child to verbalize feelings would be more appropriate.

The boundary lessons at this age are just as important to future development as the previous boundary of "I am." It is the importance of guiding the development of the balanced internal knowing of right and wrong without debilitating guilt. It is with love, understanding and limits that the child's developing initiative is preserved without sacrificing the development of conscience in the process.

It is during this time that the child develops the ability to create and learns to be creative from joyful play. Through the conflict and rivalry with siblings and playmates, the child learns to forcefully reinforce developing identity, resolve conflicts, share, develop communication skills, identify feelings and fully develop initiative which will benefit self and the world as an adult.

What I Can Do And What I Offer Is Of Value To My World

Trees

by K. Craig

ponderosa pine
i picked you out
at the tree farm
i brought you home
along with my badge that said
"be nice to a tree today"
i was so proud of you
and me

out of the plastic cup
your roots grew
tamped in the ground

near the fence of dogwood
i didn't know you'd get so big
we were
so small

you grew and
grew and
grew

we'd sit on the patio
nana and me
and talk
about daphne and geraniums
when to plant the garden
how big you were getting
what a nice tree you were
to have around
to look at

you grew so tall you
became the neighbor's view
mom decided to use your top
for a christmas tree
so we brought you into the house
that winter

we were kin
comrades
weathered survivors
we shared history
invisibly bonded
I cared for you
and I loved you
we grew up together

last week
in the driveway
i came upon you

chopped to bits
stripped of dignity

shocked and sickened
my eyes took in
your graveless corpse
piles of neatly stacked
severed limbs
bare branches
broken twigs
surrounded
by still green leaves
scattered
on blacktop

you lay
drawn and quartered
bleeding sap
aching   oozing   parched
dying

the child within me
unable to make sense of
this massacre
withdrew
into silence

words could not grasp
thoughts not assemble
reason

overwhelmed
the child within
numb
no consolation
for sixteen years of
life together
struggles reflected
growth extracted from
common soil

Vic

Vic painfully remembered the time in childhood when he was first introduced to the world of community and school.

"I couldn't speak English and had difficulty learning what was taught. My parents were poor immigrants, and I learned very quickly that I would receive no assistance at home. I had to help *them* understand the new world rather than their helping me. My mother and father both worked extremely hard. It was difficult for them to just make ends meet. I know they were in pain. I also realized then, for the first time, that my family was different and would always be different. I think I was ashamed of them and myself. The most painful time I remember was when I had to walk to the showers at school in front of all those other kids. Those who didn't have indoor hot water and bathtubs had to take showers at school. It was as if they thought we were dirty. We weren't!"

Thelma

Thelma had great difficulty with motivation.

"It seems that I can't finish anything. I just get started, then I sit down and drink a cup of coffee. I feel like such a failure. I've always been a failure."

Thelma described the feelings she had as a child of eight. "I was extremely shy in school. I never fit in somehow. It seemed like the other kids just knew how to do things. I didn't. I even felt like a visitor in my own home. My mother never let me do anything. She did all the work and complained about it. She even cleaned my room. I'd want to help so bad, but when I would, I didn't do things right, not the way she did them. I always screwed up. She said it was easier to do it herself. I'd ask for help on my homework and I'd even screw that up. She would end up doing it for me. I remembered once getting my picture in the local paper for a project my mother actually did. I was so ashamed. It was like I was an imposter. I'm still an imposter."

George

George, at 35, considered himself lazy and had extreme difficulty with procrastination. He was about to lose his job because of failure to complete projects assigned, even when they were near completion.

"It's just like it's always been. My teachers said I was lazy and I always got sent to the principal for my bad attitude. I'd get punished at home for not doing my assignments in school. My parents said I was just lazy and stubborn. I remembered once I was grounded for a whole year over school work. Why didn't I just do it? I barely graduated from high school. Now I have the same problem. I just about finish something at work, and, would you believe it, I make paper airplanes and fly them across the room instead of finishing the job. I've got a family to support, for God's sake. Now my son is just like me. He won't even pick up his room no matter how I punish him. He's just lazy and good-for-nothing like his old man."

I asked George to receive testing for learning disabilities. It was discovered that he was severely dyslexic, so considering the extent of his disability, it was an extreme achievement that he had learned to read as well as he had.

At the age of five or six, a child leaves the world of family to enter the world of school and community. It is in this new world that children are confronted with new challenges and lessons. [The tasks of "Industry vs. Inferiority" (Erikson, 1963).] Vic, Thelma and George learned through their experiences that they were "different," inferior to others and had little of value to offer to their world. Vic became a compulsive over-achiever, fighting to escape the family he left behind in the morning. He suffered constantly from survival guilt for the split loyalties between family and outside community. Thelma continued the shy and withdrawn pattern already developed in her family. As an adult she suffered severe panic attacks whenever she entered a new situation. George lost job after job for failure to complete tasks. He considered himself "no good" and continued projecting that legacy on to his son.

> "There is danger threatening the individual and society when the school-age child begins to feel that the color of his skin, the background of his parents or the fashion of his clothes, rather than his wish and will to learn, will decide his worth as an apprentice, and thus his sense of identity."
>
> Erikson, 1963

Other dangers facing children of this age develop when the way they learn does not match with the way schools teach. Many extremely bright kids with unscreened perceptual handicaps become lost in misperceived numbers and letters. Children do not know that they see or hear differently from other children and often label themselves "stupid" because they are unable to catch up. Frequently they either vanish in the back of the room or become behavior problems.

As one young man told me, "I guess it was easier to be 'bad' than 'stupid'. If I was acting out, at least I was in charge of that."

These children often experience double punishment. Parents, hearing the words of teachers, put more and more pressure on their perceived "lazy" child, intensifying the resistance and the low self-image.

The child of a compulsive workaholic or perfectionist also suffers new difficulty at this stage of development. Given the message that they have nothing to offer family or community, while their mother and dad are perfect and worthwhile, they feel themselves to be somehow defective. They may not be allowed to join the family, may have their homework done for them by someone smarter, may be shamed for the B because it is not an A or only shown their mistakes and not their successes.

Shirley

Shirley, age six, worked long and hard at school on a project for her mom for Mother's Day. She had carefully designed, fired, painted and glazed a ceramic leaf, then wrapped it, even putting one of her own hair ribbons on the package. When the special day arrived and she presented her precious gift, the first thing her mother saw was the hair ribbon.

"How many times have I told you, dear, these are only for your hair. Now look, it's all ruined." Her mom opened the gift while continuing to talk about the ribbon. When she saw the gift, she said, "Oh Shirley, that's lovely," then quickly placed it aside, "but you know what would really make Mom happy on Mother's Day. Listen to me and keep your room and your things nice. Money doesn't grow on trees, you know."

Shirley's current partner complains about her "unbearable anxiety" during the holidays and the extreme amounts of money she spends on "just the right present." Her boss grows tired of her continual apologies for her work.

Children learn their relative worth to community and world during this stage of development. They need to learn that what they do is valuable. They also need to be able to make mistakes, correct them and ultimately succeed in their own style of learning. It is extremely important for all children, including those of racial or ethnic minorities, those with handicaps, perceptual or economic differences, to have a supportive environment in school and at home to teach them to deal with the prejudices they are bound to face in the world and to teach them the skills to succeed in the face of differences.

For children who have suffered shame and guilt in past developmental periods, this stage of development may bring mixed blessings. They may experience success for the first time in this new world outside home and continue to an even greater extent to forfeit their true self to an image acceptable to those around them.

Those children who suffer lack of success or worth in their accomplishments at this stage of development may learn that what they have to offer their world is of little value. Children who did not learn early lessons of trust, pride in autonomy and self-confidence in early initiative, might feel true success in industry. They may, however, wait for the applause from their world to fill an empty space inside them that simply cannot be filled in the world of work alone.

Who Am I? Can I Leave You Without Losing You? Can I Be With You Without Losing Me?

Stewart Family

The Stewart brothers seemed to create interest with neighbors and family friends. They ranged in age from 13 to 18. The four were mannerly, verbal and had strong opinions. Each was very different from the other in personality, dress and interests, and each had his own peer group with whom he spent time.

Jim, the oldest, liked to wear jeans, sweatshirts, loose jackets (usually with a peace sign painted on it somewhere) and hats of every possible type and description. His hair was short and conservative. He loved the Beatles, Bogart and all the early comedians. He had definite views on politics, was an avid reader, loved adventure and was into world peace and saving every animal that was going to become extinct. His room was decorated with Charlie Chaplin, Bogart and Beatle posters, clippings on one movement or another, animal posters (especially otters) and was usually "messy."

The second brother, Ben, was quiet, humorous and artistic. He loved rock groups, especially Kiss, and had a passion for eagles. He had long curly hair, wore black "rock shirts," black jeans and black sneakers. His ambition was to become an artist and from an early age, he spent many hours a day painting and drawing. He also loved pets and had a bird that reluctantly learned to talk and whistle. His room was decorated with "rock" and eagle posters, his own art work, a painting and sitting area, and his bird. He was sometimes neat and sometimes messy, depending on his interests for the week.

Mike, the third brother, was into style. His hair fluctuated from short to "new wave," short with longer spikes, sometimes parts of it were bleached or dyed. He dressed in stylish slacks, button-down shirts of all colors, sweaters and shoes (instead of sneakers). His room was filled with tones of color, mirrors, flamingos, artistic paintings (especially Nagel) and pictures of friends. He had a small sitting area and his room was neat and clean. He liked order. His musical preference was mostly popular and "wave," his favorite group being Cure. He enjoyed creative writing, painting and science.

The youngest brother, Todd, fluctuated in dress from blue jeans and jean jackets to "rock shirts" and black Levis. His hair was straight, long in back and short in front. He loved stuffed animals and ceramic animal figurines (especially deer). His passions included athletics, video games, his bicycle, rock music, and chameleons. His usually tidy but cluttered room reflected all of these interests. He was not yet sure what he wanted to do as an adult, but he thought being a lawyer was a good idea.

Two of the brothers were quieter with others than they were with family, whereas the other two were verbal in all settings. All four talked incessantly at the dinner table. Each went through the various developmental stages very differently from one another.

The Stewart parents, as is usually the case, received varying reactions to their child-rearing practices from family, friends and neighbors. Some thought the boys "delightful" and loved their differences and the child centeredness of the home. Others thought they were nice kids but were aghast at the allowances the older Stewarts made in terms of dress styles. Comments included, "Why doesn't he cut his hair?" or "Don't you think that color is a bit much?" or "Do they always talk that much at dinner? What about the adults in the house?" To this Mrs. Stewart would reply, "It's not my hair, as long as it's clean and neat, he can wear it as he likes. I stress the big things, like care and respect for self and others." To this an extended family member once replied, "Well, I don't think long hair is respectful to anyone!" Others felt that way, too. Once Ben had become very angry when he had been refused a job because of his long hair. Mrs. Stewart told him that as an adult he might have trouble with other jobs because of his hairstyle. Ben was shocked by that comment and replied, "Mother, for heavens sake, I'm not going to be wearing my hair this way as an adult. I'm just an adolescent."

Ben's words were backed by behavior. Much to his family's surprise, when Ben was 17, he appeared at the door one day with his hair cut short. His selection of clothing soon matched the change of hairstyle.

The onset of puberty and adolescence is an extremely confusing time of development and a time when new lessons are learned and old ones tested and relearned. The major tasks of adolescents are to learn the lessons of their growing sexuality, i.e., learn the differences between sex and nurturing and take responsibility for both needs and behavior. They struggle with "Who am I?" and have the task of integrating experiments in the present, the world of peers, with lessons learned in their early years. This is necessary in order to attain new confidence in who they are in relationship to others. They struggle constantly with independence and dependence because they face separation from the family in terms of leaving home. Support for this struggle involves allowing development of interests, causes and relationships, while still setting limits that involve safety. It also involves supporting both independence and dependence so that the lessons can be learned that in intimate relationships both are acceptable. The adolescent without limits fights and acts out to get them. The adolescent with too many restrictions fights for independence.

"Winnicott saw in adolescence a time when a new adaptation to reality has to be made when the vulnerability of the self causes a new necessity for dependence. The problems of the adolescent boy or girl could be said to center around the statement 'I am' and the question 'what am I?' Without an answer to this question, it is difficult to feel real, for the capacity to feel real is itself a result of self-discovery."

Davis and Wallbridge, 1981

I Am Five

by Nanci Presley-Holley

I am 5.
Daddy you are hurting me.
You touch me in ways I don't understand.
Are all fathers this way?
Do my friends' fathers touch them?
"Don't tell, trust me.
This is right.
Mother will blame you."
Alcohol breath,
his closeness I abhor.
I hate you, daddy.
Die.

I am 6.
Why doesn't ma-ma stop him?
Our house is small,
doesn't she hear?
Everyone must know —
Isn't it written on my forehead?
"Don't tell, you are to blame."

I am 7.
If I don't breathe
when he comes to my room,
I will be invisible
and the pain will cease.

I stand next to my dad,
He lies so still.
Is he breathing?
Drunk, he's drunk.
Die, you bastard, die.

My dad is ill.
He doesn't drink now.
He doesn't touch me in that secret way.
Is this reality?
Am I sane?

Oh God, oh God, oh God!
My daddy died.
Are you punishing me?
This is the man I came to love.
Why have you taken him from me?
Is it because of the secret?

Am I that powerful
To wish death?
Is it my fault?
I am only 8
Please God bring him back.

Ma-ma says, "Don't cry."
So, I hide.
I will not feel this pain.
I have been taught well.
Silence.

I am 37.
If time heals all wounds
Then why do I bleed?
Still.

I come to this place.
It is warm, it is safe.
Loving hands reach out,

Let go, trust, feel, talk.
We will carry part of the burden now.

Hold me, rock me.
Don't let me go.
I am afraid.
I will die if I tell.
Why do I feel 5?

To talk, to breathe
Let the fear and pain subside
Write about it.
Talk about it.
Scream about it.
Cry about it.
Grieve.
For the lost childhood.

I am 38
I am angry.
I feel.
I trust.
I am no longer a secret.
But who am I now?

I am 5.
I am a little girl.
I am a young woman.
I am . . .

(Reprinted from *Bread and Roses,*
Health Communications, 1988.)

Many adults with whom I work have said that they have never gone through adolescence, then pause and ask, "Is that possible?" Yes, it is possible, and in fact probable in families where parents are themselves survivors of unresolved trauma. This question is usually asked in therapy after the individual, through griefwork, has separated and developed an internal boundary of "I am." The realization then comes that they have little idea of their own interests, likes or dislikes. Without feeling a sense of self, they could never explore who that self was in normal adolescent years. The parents who must have a child dressed in a particular way, who cannot tolerate differences of opinion, who open mail and search through an adolescent's personal belongings or depends upon the child inappropriately to meet their own needs for connectedness, ego or belonging, have never allowed the child's autonomous separation. These parents have never been able to progress fully through developmental stages or feel solidity in their own boundary development.

Adolescence has been delayed for many adults, not only because of an inability to fully achieve the autonomy of emotional boundary development, but because they had their physical boundaries violated as well. These individuals go through life never learning the lessons so important in this adolescent period, that nurturing and sexuality are not the same thing. Often they end up having their own physical boundaries violated, violating those of others, living their lives in isolation to protect against further abuse or never experiencing the joys of their own fully developed sexuality.

Ann

Ann said that both of her parents were alcoholic from the time she was born. She felt from an early age that her mother wished she had never been born.

"Mom was always so distant, so shaming, so cold." She felt much closer to her father who was her major nurturer. She remembered that he was warm and caring and that when she would sit on his lap as a small child, she always felt loved.

According to Ann, she was always aware of the distance between her parents. Then her father confided in her when she was 10 that they never had sex because her mother would not allow it. From an early age, Ann said, she would listen to her parents fight late at night.

These fights were always about her and her brother. Her dad would defend Ann while her mother would attack Ann and defend her brother. Ann said her mother had total control and would always win the fights. The fights stopped when her mom started working days and her dad worked nights.

"They rarely saw each other when I got to be about 10. Things seemed better for a while."

When Ann was about 11, the affection between her and her father changed. After school her dad would cuddle her as he had before, but also started caressing her legs and then would "rub higher." She said she felt awkward but did not know why. She loved the touch but hated the feelings she had.

Ann related that she was responsible for all the housekeeping chores after mother started work.

"If it wasn't done perfectly, white glove clean, I'd really get it." Her dad would help her with the housework, then when it was finished he would cuddle her on the couch. "He always gave my brother errands to do and money to spend on comics or the movies." Then when Ann's brother was out of the house, her dad would show her his penis and ask her to touch it.

"My body began to develop when I was about 12. I tried to hide it. I always wore loose clothes, dark colors, 'cause Dad noticed my body. He was always commenting on how beautiful I was. He said I was just like him." Pausing, Ann then said, "I liked being special, you know, being told I was beautiful, but it made me feel so uncomfortable. I thought he was watching me all the time. Then one morning I was awakened by him standing next to my bed. He was, ah, rubbing his penis on my mouth. It terrified me! This was my dad!" Ann began to cry.

She said that she then started sleeping in the bathtub. It was cold but the bathroom had the only door in the house that locked. When her mother got up to get ready for work, she would get mad at Ann for the locked door.

'She always asked me what I was doing in there. I felt so ashamed."

Ann felt extreme guilt over what she called "her part in the abuse." When she was 13, her father would offer her favors for "touching him" and letting him rub against her. He would do her housework, give her money for clothes, let her go out with friends. Ann said that each time this happened, she always promised herself it would be the last time. She also noticed that when she was "good" to her father, things seemed to go better at home. He always told Ann that her mom just would not "help him out" and she understood because her mother would not help her either.

She said that she did try to tell her mother about it when she was 15, but her mom would not believe her. Her mother told her that she was confusing her father with the "bad boys" she was hanging out with.

In late adolescence, Ann said, she learned that her brother was being abused by her mother. She had walked into her brother's room and found her mother lying next to him in bed. She had never talked to her brother about this.

Ann left home at 18. She was proud that she was still a virgin for that meant that she was still a "good girl." She would never let a boy touch her and felt uncomfortable dating. At 21 she married a man who "never tried anything." She said that he seemed as frightened of sex as she was and that most of the time after the marriage they were distant.

At age 24 Ann became extremely ill with ulcers that a doctor diagnosed as having started years before. She was also severely depressed and went to a therapist for the first time. Ann built enough of a relationship with the counselor to tell her about the sexual abuse from her father. Even though she had never discussed it with her brother, she told the therapist about his abuse by their mother. According to Ann, the only thing the therapist said was, "It happens in a lot of families."

"She ignored it. So did I. I felt that old sense of shame. I never went back to see her."

Still plagued by depression, Ann went to another therapist when she was 26. "He was great. He held me when I cried just like my dad would when I was a little girl. I fell in love with him. We ended up dating and making love. I left my husband, but he never left his wife, so it ended."

At age 29, Ann attempted suicide. She came into counseling at that time. When asked about the history of abuse in her family, Ann replied, "You have to understand, I loved my father and I hated him. I desperately wanted my mother's love, but I hated her. I'm so confused. Please don't misunderstand, my dad loves me." It took Ann a long time to realize that she had been re-abused by others in her life, including the therapist. She felt she had seduced him and that the affair was her fault. She had, at that time, decided to live in isolation, afraid to trust others because she could not depend on her ability to trust herself. She had never experienced an orgasm and had decided never to raise children because, "I feel like a child myself."

During puberty Ann had been sexually abused by the parent who had given her the most nurturing, thus confusing sexuality and nurturing. She was never allowed to develop her own physical or emotional boundaries internally. The therapist nurtured her, therefore, sexuality in her mind followed. If she enjoyed a sexual experience, or her own sexuality, that meant she was really a "bad girl" after all, resulting in the need to repress all sexual desires. She also repressed her anger at her father because being angry meant that she would also have to give up the nurturing parent who she loved and on whom she depended.

Ann was terrified of relationships during adolescence, afraid that if someone in a relationship wanted sex, she had to say yes. She felt she had no choices if she accepted a date for a movie or dinner. If she went out, she could not keep an image of herself as a "good girl."

For other victims of abuse, adolescence becomes a time of sexual promiscuity, feeling that "being an object" is all they know how to do to be accepted or worthwhile. They have never learned the skills of forming different types of relationships and have learned that sex is the price you pay for any nurturing by others.

Covert abuse is just as damaging during this period of development. Being "Mommy's man" or "Daddy's woman" leads to great difficulty in this period of separation.

> "Children fused to a lonely parent may grow up and marry but unless they have 'divorced' that parent, the marriage may well fail. The relationship vacuum may be filled with drink, compulsive behavior, or another cross-generational relationship. The opportunity for mature relationships has been cut off in each generation."
>
> Fossum and Mason, 1986

Adolescence is a period of integrating "who I am." It is a stage of exploration, battling limits and experimenting with choices. These are the years for following peers, yet learning to assert self in light of group pressure. It is a time of wrestling internally with new feelings of sexuality and learning the difference between nurturing and sex. This is the period for seeking new interests, goals and style while holding on to old lessons learned in the family. The struggle for autonomy was a period of holding on and at the same time letting go. Puberty and adolescence is a time of being dependent one minute and independent the next, a time of separation and building identity.

A friend of mine once likened it to driving a Cadillac with a Kiddy Car steering wheel. Erikson (1963) states that the lessons to be learned at this stage are identity versus role confusion.

For many parents and adolescents this is the most difficult stage of development. Those who spent their adolescent years in a boarding school will find it difficult to know how to parent their children through this stage.

Individuals who were in a concentration camp, the major ambassador to the new world for immigrant parents, fighting in a war or suffering the poverty of the Depression during their own adolescent years, may see their adolescents as "spoiled," "bratty" or "becoming fresh like all those other American middle-class kids." They may set tighter limits and suffer more rebellion as a result. Some parents cannot allow for separation because of their own unmet needs. Others will want to be a "buddy" instead of a parent, and the adolescent will have to push even harder to get boundaries to fight against.

Many kids will go into adolescence unprepared, without fully having learned the lessons of trust, autonomy, initiative or successes in industry. Too many will skip this learning stage altogether because it is a luxury that kids with family stressors, such as alcoholism, poverty, catastrophic illness, pain of immigration, violence, cultural self-hate, emotional or sexual abuse, cannot afford. They will instead spend their energy or repression of needs and growing sexuality and on simply surviving.

Adolescents with the highest rate of suicide, drug and alcohol abuse and pregnancy are frequently those with the lowest scores on verbal ability. They cannot communicate needs, feelings, goals, ideas or thoughts. Many of these adolescents have extremely high scores in tests of factual knowlege (Glenn, 1988). These were kids who with all their acquired knowledge have never learned, "I am. I can have and can express my own feelings without being hurt or hurting others. What I have to offer is of value in my world and to whom and what I am."

I have read many accounts in various local newspapers of the shocked responses of communities to adolescents who have graduated from high school with straight A's, received countless scholarships, been popular good kids and who have committed suicide the summer after graduation. With all their learned knowledge, they could not communicate their pain to others. There has been an epidemic of suicides among adolescent Native American males on reservations and in villages. Many of these young men saw no future and felt they had nothing to offer to their world. They, too, had learned no way to fully communicate their sense of helplessness and pain.

The Development Of Boundaries: A Review

Each infant comes into the world completely dependent. The task in just 18 short years is to learn lessons that will allow an independent young adult to leave home, develop a network of supportive friends, feel autonomy yet commitment in intimate relationships, develop a career and earn a living, possess interest in community and feel value in the world, be responsible to self and others, parent emotionally healthy children, face traumas, grieve losses, experience joy, face death.

The infant does not learn these lessons through some inborn knowledge or merely by putting in time, although many people I have worked with have expected that of themselves. They learn through patient, loving, limit-setting, consistent parents who have themselves been able to learn the lessons. Parents who have fully developed, positive, autonomous identities and resulting internal boundaries are able to nurture the healthy development of autonomous identities and internal boundaries in their children.

Parents who experience unresolved traumas in their own developmental years or who have faced severe unresolved traumas that have caused regression in development, will continually attempt resolution through their children, will require their children to parent them, will not be able to bond, will have anxious attachments to their children or will require the child to function as an unresolved or disowned part of themselves. The child, therefore, will be required to be a part of the parent, rather than being nurtured in the development of self. The energy spent on repression of parts of the self (anger, needs, joy, personal power, sexuality, for example) is energy that cannot be expended on further development. Internal conflicts, such as the need for independence versus dependence or anger versus compliance, lead to repression of one side or the other of the conflict. This repression and denial of the original struggle creates continual underlying anxiety that frequently results in phobias, physical illnesses, debilitating depression and compulsive behaviors during adulthood. For Vic, at the beginning of this section, one underlying conflict may be loyalty to his family versus success and happiness in the new world.

It is my belief that human beings continually strive toward health rather than illness. Children who suffer trauma to core self and identity, therefore, work toward resolution of that trauma and to completion of development in adult life through repetition of the struggle with authority figures, in intimate relationships, through their own children or in therapy.

Wilber (1981) said that the boundary between self and not-self is the first one we draw and the last one we erase. Infants in the first few months of life, through the consistence, care and love of parents, learn to internalize that loving consistent care enough to develop self-confidence and security in brief times alone. This learned ability to trust in parent, then self, becomes the first step in developing a boundary between "not me" and "me." It is the ability to self-soothe and spend time alone with the security that someone is always there inside.

With the trust learned in this all-important first stage, the child of nine months to a year old learns for the first time that he is a separate person. The child has learned "I am," the second internal boundary. Hopefully, with loving protective support from the parent, the toddler will learn that it is all right to explore autonomously and return, be interested and active, as well as quiet and held.

Around the end of the first year and the beginning of the second year, is another extremely important step in boundary development. The child's task, which starts at this age and continues at different levels through adolescence, is the development of an internal sense of right and wrong, conscience and empathy for others. It is one of the most difficult stages for parents who have unresolved issues in their own development and need the child as parent or part of themselves because it involves the child's emotional self as separate from them. At this stage the child needs to learn that they can be angry, have personal power, needs and independent desires without being injured or abandoned and without injuring or debilitating the parent. If the parent allows for the child's emotions and separate desires, while lovingly guiding their expression with limits, the child as an adult will have a loving, yet firm conscience.

For example, "I can understand your anger at your new baby brother, but you need to talk to me about it. I won't let you hit him."

The child at this age also needs to be able to repair conflicts with the parent, which will later evolve into the adult's ability for empathy and conflict resolution in relationships.

For example, "I'm sorry I got so mad, Mommy."

"I know. I'm sorry, too. We were both mad, weren't we. Let's talk about it."

Compare the response with the parent that cannot tolerate the child's expression of feelings: "I'm sorry I got so mad, Mommy."

"No you're not! You're never sorry. You made me sick and now I hope you're happy!"

The latter may produce a child who has to repress all of her angry feelings in order to survive. She will learn that feelings are more powerful than life and can injure those around them. As adults, they will suffer the consequences of that repression.

But a child with few limits on behavior, such as having a parent who would allow the child to hit her, may have to prematurely develop extreme internal limits on self, or as an adult continually need limits from the outside. This emotional abandonment of the parent can lead to a person continually acting out who still uses the external world for a conscience, or to a person who must fuse with others.

With the onset of school age the child has still another lesson to learn. The child entering the world of school and community moves from, "I am a person whose feelings and needs are important" to "I am a person who has something of value to offer in this world."

Frequently, for childen with "differences" (such as racial or ethnic minorities, children of immigrants who have difficulty with language, children who have perceptual handicaps or physical disabilities), this may be an extremely devastating experience. If school teachers and other personnel ignore differences in learning styles, or are unable to value and respect different cultures and economic backgrounds, they may fail to aid the child's peer group in accepting the value of all individuals. They may also have preconceived ideas or prejudices regarding the child's motivation and label the child lazy or a behavior problem. The child may learn from this experience that she is stupid, dirty or lazy and has little to contribute.

It is important for children of this age to have permeable boundaries between home and school. The child needs to bring home and receive support, acceptance and guidance in their initial ventures into the world of industry and community. Children from families where parents are undergoing the stress of differences or who have not resolved their own issues of childhood prejudice and trauma, may not offer assistance to the struggling child. They may inadvertently give the message, "We can't help you; don't ask" or "You'll never suffer as much as we have; your needs cannot be important." The child may feel a rigid boundary between home and school (children who see and feel extreme differences in lifestyles, values or functioning) and may develop a split in loyalties between family and community. This child may feel the need to find acceptance in the broader world, yet not let themselves achieve pleasure fully due to survival guilt or cultural self-hate.

For some children the worth is also devalued at home by parents who expect and need perfection, do not value the child's growing abilities, do their homework for them or never let them contribute to the family. The parents may unknowingly accept the words of teachers regarding the child's learning style differences.

The world of school is the first success felt in life for some children. It is where they attempt to make up for lack of self-esteem through rewards in achievement.

Adolescence brings on new developmental tasks to be learned, as well as the need to reaffirm old developmental lessons. During this period, the child, now a young adult, struggles with the need to be both dependent and independent and the need to explore interests, relationships, and causes. It is also a time for using old skills in new, more independent ways, developing the boundary between nurturing and sexuality.

As it is at age two, adolescence is a period when the individual needs both freedom of expression and protective limits, with an emphasis on *letting go* with guidance. An adolescent who perceives that the parent's needs supersede her own will not be able to go through this important period of exploring who she is or practice skills for independence.

The adolescents without limits to push against will continue escalating their behavior to get limits. The adolescent who is not allowed the freedom of expression in values, style, dress or interests because of overly strict parents will need to rebel even stronger to separate. The adolescent who is overtly or covertly sexually abused will have few and poorly defined boundaries between nurturance and sexuality. They will frequently end up being repeatedly abused, abuse others without being aware of a boundary or will isolate in order to impose a protective boundary. They may also experience the extreme internal conflicts between sexual needs and being good. Repressing one side of this conflict will often result in suppression of their sexuality or acting-out behavior. The abused adolescent may well experience another internal conflict, anger at the abuse versus keeping the nurturing parent. This frequently leads to denial of the abuse and self-blame.

The important lesson of identity in adolescence could be expressed by the following:

> "I need to find out who I am."
> "I need to know that I can leave you without losing you."
> "Can I be with you without losing me?"

Boundaries And Therapy

Individuals who have not been able to complete developmental stages and establish internal boundaries will continue to struggle for resolution in adult life. Many will attempt this completion in therapy. Unfortunately a lack of understanding about boundary development or the therapist's own lack of completion in this area frequently leads to more failure in the therapy experience for many individuals.

The therapist who is not consistent in contracted scheduling or who is overwhelmingly "there" does not aid the individual in learning self-trust and self-soothing. If the therapist cannot tolerate expressions of resistance or needs to have a constantly "growing" client, he is not aiding the individual in separation. Many individuals I have treated have been given ultimatums by previous therapists to leave self-destructive relationships or discontinue therapy. These individuals are not aiding the client in exploring that emotional attachment, the unresolved trauma of earlier attachments or supporting the client's growth of a separate self. Professionals who cannot allow the expression of feelings toward them, either through verbal or nonverbal cues, are inadvertently reinforcing the individual's belief that emotional expression is dangerous.

This may also happen when the therapist, by omission, does not bring up issues regarding the therapeutic relationship. When the therapist joins the client in the belief that the therapist is the only one who can "cure" her, becomes angry at the individual's acting-out behavior or does not set boundaries and limits on behavior in the therapeutic relationship, the therapist is not aiding the client in the development of self-control.

Although it is controversial, I also feel that behavioral control or medication management alone are insufficient for symptoms such as panic attacks. These approaches inadvertently support image development, reinforce repression of emotional pain, neglecting once again the frightened child inside.

When a therapist avoids cultural, ethnic or perceptual differences, he may also inadvertently be giving credence to an individual's feelings of powerlessness or worthlessness.

A therapist who ignores or avoids abuse issues by not asking about them, frequently reinforces shame and repression. The therapist who makes friends or begins intimate relationships with clients is recreating the abuse dynamic. Likewise, therapists who focus only on the abuse and not the nurturing needs that have been met may be ignoring an important value to the individual. This can result in further repression of one side of the internal conflict. Or it may instead force, as was the case in the incest dynamic, a choice in loyalty between one individual (in this case the therapist) or the other (the abusive parent).

Currently, there are those individuals in the profession who serve as self-appointed "boundary-mounties." It is important to protect a potential client against an abusive parent or professional. It is also important not to let our needs supersede the client's. In some cases the focus on punishment rather than seeking safety, limits and treatment, may supersede the client's need for resolution and growth. This need for punishment may well be the professional's need for resolution rather than focus and concern for the client's best interests.

Boundaries develop through loving consistency and respect for a separate human being. Individuals who have not been supported in the completion of developmental stages often believe they failed at growing up and punish themselves in one way or another for the emotional and psychological pain and neglect they suffered. They expect themselves to have learned lessons they were never taught. Or they expect to be able to parent children perfectly when they were never parented adequately themselves.

I truly believe all individuals seek health and continually attempt effective resolution.

S. A. Harris

T H R E E

Panic Attacks:
A Window To The Frightened Child

Warrior Child

by Nanci Presley-Holley

I've never been a soldier
But I know what war is like
Having survived a childhood
Besieged by enemies
More dangerous and insidious
Than those
Armies face with guns
My foes were alcoholism and child abuse

And I was unarmed
I never got just the one-year tour of duty

In some battle-torn country
I was there for the duration
from birth to age 18
Escaping like a prisoner of war
Only to be snapped back into the fold
When they'd find out where I lived
Or I broke down and told

Just like a soldier who has no life of his own
I was my family's possession
Theirs to send where they wished
Sometimes to grandma's, an aunt's, an uncle's
When the burden of raising three children
Pushed them to the limit
But it wasn't "rest and relaxation" for me
'Cause no matter where I went
The disease ran rampant
Through my family

"Army issue" was hand me downs
Or poorly made clothes by a woman
Trying to maintain her sanity
'Cause dad had drank up what little money there was
Or spent it on some floozy in town

Bedroom inspections were always on Saturday
If everything was perfect
We could go outside for the day
But a comic book out of place
    or a messy bed
We'd pay dearly
What does a five year old really know
About dust and hospital corners?

Normal childhood activities, like play?
Not this child
I was always combat ready
Training myself to survive
I had to be on guard, alert

For the fist in the stomach, a slap upside the head
Because I'd spoken when I was supposed to be quiet
Or asked for something to eat
Or even colored over the lines
I never knew when the flak would hit
There was never any warning
I wished there'd been someone
To scream "incoming"

Nighttime was the worst
But unlike armed camps
There weren't any sentries
Laying in my bed
Hovering between exhaustion and sleep
Listening for the whisper of the intruder
Just in case he crept toward my room
Or waking to find he'd already infiltrated
And was laying on top of me
How could I do anything else
. . . Except play dead?

My childhood was a war zone
As frightening and devastating as Viet Nam
A battleground of fear
Where discord and conflict were the rule
Once in a while
When I allow the feelings stored since childhood
To bubble to the surface
I have a hard time keeping them under control
I immediately want to fight or flee
Destroy something
Sometimes
  Even
   Me

Grace

Grace referred herself to therapy when she was 28.
She had suffered from severe panic attacks for three

years. During that time she had gone to many medical specialists, including a psychiatrist. Her attacks typically involved hyperventilation, heart palpitations, chest pains and intense anxiety to the point of panic following any aerobic exercise. With each attack, she believed that she was going to die. She had spent thousands of dollars on cardiovascular tests and complete physicals. Medical specialists always told her that she was in excellent physical health. After each round of tests she would relax a bit, then start her own research into the problem. After reading countless medical textbooks and journals, finding many possible rare conditions, Grace would test herself and have another attack. She would then see another doctor, armed with the names of new possible causes for her condition. One doctor referred her to a psychiatrist who gave her a prescription of Xanex, a tranquilizer used in the medical treatment of panic attacks. The medications relieved her symptoms to some degree, but the attacks persisted.

Grace was an attractive, pleasant, competent, articulate woman. In keeping with her pattern, she arrived at our first session with a recent medical journal which she felt revealed a new plausible reason for her symptoms.

"I'm really not resistant to trying therapy," she said intently, "but I don't think my condition is psychological. It feels physical. I think it is serious. I'm afraid one of these days I might die while looking for psychological answers. I know I'm not crazy."

I told her that I was not a physician, that if it made her more comfortable, she should continue receiving medical care from her doctor during our work together. I also explained that severe anxiety attacks do cause physical symptoms, including the ones she had mentioned. I assured her that I could understand her fear and the incredible discomfort she must be feeling, but even if her attacks were the result of anxiety, that certainly did not mean she was "crazy." She seemed to relax in her chair and placed the medical journal on the table next to her.

"You mean you don't mind if I continue to check out possible medical causes while I'm working with you?"

It was stressed that what I wanted was in her best interest, that finding the cause and alleviating the painful attacks were most important.

"Should I continue taking this medication? It seems to help."

I explained that I was not in favor of the use of tranquilizers and was concerned about possible addiction. I told her again that I was not a medical doctor and that while she was under the care of her own psychiatrist, I would need a signed release so I could discuss my concerns with him as well. She agreed, then explained that she had become fearful of stopping the medication. She also told me that she had requested a small dose because she did not like the idea of becoming dependent on medications.

The initial interviews with Grace revealed that her "attacks" had begun shortly before graduating from law school. She had been very athletic in high school and college and was fine during that period of her life. She also told me that during her last year of law school she had begun a relationship with the man to whom she was now married and that was "the best thing that had ever happened" in her life. Later sessions revealed, however, that her husband was very "bossy." But she did not allow herself expression of any anger in the relationship because, "He doesn't mean to be so domineering and it would kill him if he ever thought I was unhappy with him."

Grace told me that her father was alcoholic during her growing up years but that he was now in recovery. She said, however, that his drinking had not really affected her that much because her mother took charge of everything. Both of Grace's parents had immigrated from Sweden and were very tough, stoic people who had little use for emotions. She also added, "You're just supposed to work hard and take life as it comes. They would think my coming to see you was frivolous and expensive. They'd just work harder."

"What do you think?"

"I don't know. I've tried so hard controlling it. It's strange; I've never been afraid of anything in my life. As a kid I always did all kinds of things. I was a real risk-taker. That's why I think my problem is physical. I'm still not afraid of things. I don't give in to emotions. I just don't want to die. I've got my whole life to live."

Grace was the youngest of two siblings. She said she was the strong one and that her brother had been "sickly" from birth. She was in charge of watching over her brother who had suffered from severe childhood asthma. She told me that he had been killed at age ten, when Grace was nine.

"It was my job to watch him. I didn't mind, though. I loved him. We did everything together. I was the 'strong one'. He couldn't help it; he was sick. I felt sorry for him. Mother told me I had been put on earth to keep Mark safe. He was so good. I never got angry with him except the morning he died." She became very stoic, yet looked confused.

"You know, I've never talked about this. It's funny; I don't think anyone has even asked. My family, even Tom [her husband], believes what's past is past. I guess I felt guilty. I don't know. I was supposed to watch him. Nobody ever blamed me though. Mom and Dad never said a word about it. What happened, happened, you know?"

Grace told me that her brother had died on a Saturday in April. She couldn't remember the date. She said that her dad had been drinking, which was usual for week-ends. He worked very hard during the week and just wanted time to himself on his days off. Grace said her mother usually asked her to take Mark out of the house.

"She wouldn't want us to come back until it was getting dark and Dad had passed out. Dad wouldn't be very nice to Mark when he was drinking. He always called him 'sissy' and 'momma's boy'. He thought Mom and I protected Mark too much."

Grace explained that on this particular day, Mark had been really irritable. He did not want to leave the house because he had been working on a project and wanted to finish it.

"He was so smart. He was always doing something in his room. He got really good grades, better than mine. He was not usually that stubborn. Mom said I was the stubborn one and that it would get me in deep trouble someday." Grace said that she had fought with Mark to get him out of the house. She had been scolded for not leaving faster. "He just didn't want to go." She said that she had another fight with Mark when they left the house. He had wanted to sit and read comics in a park near their house. She had been tired of "always playing cards and reading comics" and wanted to go across town to visit a schoolfriend (which she explained that she never got to do because she was always doing school work, housework with her mother or watching Mark). Mark had said it was too far. She had told him that it would be hours before dark and that it really was not that far. She forced him to go but he resisted all the way.

According to Grace, when they got to her friend's they had a really good time. It was getting dark and they had an hour's walk home. Mark had wanted to call their mother, but she knew her mother would be furious if they did. The phone might wake her dad. Her mother never left the neighborhood and, besides, they had stayed out after dark before and Mom never seemed to mind.

While walking home through a strange neighborhood, Grace felt a man following them. "We walked faster, so did he. I began to run. I thought Mark was right behind me. I ran all the way home. Mark wasn't behind me. They didn't find his body for two days. He had been raped and killed. They found the guy, though. I know it was him, but he never got convicted. I've never forgiven that judge. I learned in law school how many loopholes there are. It's criminal. Anyway, Mother said what happened, happened. She never got mad. She has never talked about Mark since. She's never changed his room either. It's still got all his stuff in it, but she uses it as a guest room. I used to have to clean it every week. My room's the same as it was when I left, too, I guess. I never thought about that before. I guess Mom cleans both rooms now."

Grace's panic attacks began in the spring of her graduation from law school and had progressively become worse since that time. They also began when she was jogging and, when I first saw her, were occurring whenever her pulse would reach aerobic beat. The "triggers" for the onset of the attacks were the springtime (the same time of year her brother had died), increased pulse rate by running (as it had been as a child when she had run away from the man who killed her brother), her graduation from law school (which stimulated in her the same feelings of repressed anger she had toward her brother).

Sometime during the first year of treatment, in a session following a panic attack and another appointment with a specialist, I made the following interpretation to Grace.

Grace: This one was a real bad one. I feel like I'm slowly dying. I'm terrified and nobody seems to be able to find out what's wrong. (Grace was exhausted and depressed.)

Middelton-Moz: Are you sure, Grace, that part of you doesn't believe you should be dead?

Upon hearing this, Grace began sobbing. She was surprised by her tears and by the words that came through the sobs, "I should have died, not him. He was the good one."

Following this interpretation (and many others in her two and one half years of treatment) regarding the repressed conflicts and anger within her, the panic attacks decreased, then stopped. Through her descriptions of early childhood experiences, dreams, weekly journals and feelings before, during and after anxiety attacks, Grace was able to offer me a window to the frightened child inside her. With support, structure, interpretation and through building a relationship with someone willing to be present for her, Grace was able to walk slowly back through the trauma, complete developmental lessons and retrieve her discarded child.

I have never worked with an individual whose symptoms and behavior did not ultimately make sense. Symptoms, such as Grace's anxiety attacks and suppression of self in intimate relationships, eventually provided a map to her attempted resolutions of early trauma. She was attempting to complete unresolved lessons from early developmental years. It is necessary to have someone willing to listen openly, unbiased by preconceived prejudices or categories ("Listening With a Third Ear," as Theodore Reik would call it) to aid in illuminating the map toward health.

The Nature Of Anxiety

The reader might well ask at this point, "What is the difference between healthy anxiety and the panic that Grace experienced? Is anxiety healthy?" In my opinion, both are healthy but very different responses.

Rolly May (1979) makes a distinction, as did Freud, between normal anxiety and neurotic anxiety. He defines normal anxiety as "instincts of self-preservation." I would add that if normal anxiety is directed toward preservation of the self, then the latter is directed toward the preservation of the individual's identity from the effects of potentially debilitating trauma.

For instance, a child may have had a traumatic experience with a neighbor's cat. Perhaps the cat scratched the child when she was playing. Cats in the future may represent danger. When the child sees a cat, the child may experience anxiety. This "normal" anxiety may cause the child to run away.

A second child might be terrified of cats without ever having such a threatening experience. When the child sees a cat, the child panics and freezes, overwhelmed with anxiety. How do we account for the child's reaction? What is the danger or fear that the child is experiencing?

Let us imagine that this child is extremely angry at a baby brother because of all the attention this new sibling is taking away from her. When she gets angry at her brother, her mother punishes her and tells her she is a "bad girl" for having such feelings. Even though she is angry at her baby brother and mother, to express it is dangerous to a sense of security. She feels internally helpless in resolving the conflict and displaces her anger onto the cat. The cat may then represent fear of her anger and resulting fear of her mother's anger and resulting abandonment. She has more objective control regarding her fear of cats; she can avoid them. Also she may get comfort from her mom regarding this fear that she could not get in her anger toward her brother. To the child, the danger is experienced as real. It is not fear of cats (although it is experienced as such) but what the cat has come to represent internally. The degree of external fear matches her internal fear.

Red Dog

by Ruth Kane

Run Red Dog,
Get away from here.
I'm throwing rocks at you.
You are too big.
I am afraid of you.

I hear you growling,
Lurking outside the circle.
I hate you, Red Dog.
You are rage and power.
You will savage me.

> Red Dog, you do not belong at a campfire,
> Why must you always come?
> Why must you always be part of the fire?

Normal anxiety does not show itself as panic because it can be handled constructively. It is proportional to the perceived threat. It does not involve the need for defense mechanisms such as repression or displacement. Normal anxiety can be managed with conscious awareness and can be relieved when the situation is changed. In other words, normal anxiety is the result of a real danger and can be relieved if a solution can be found to protect the individual from harm. The anxiety can be soothed.

In the case of Grace, no "reality evidence" of her good health from doctors could lessen her fears. A child who has experienced a real danger from a cat can be comforted, reassured, protected and will respond positively. A child who is afraid of her anger and resulting abandonment and has displaced that anger and fear on an animal, cannot be convinced of her safety because the cat is not the real threat.

The type of anxiety that was experienced by Grace was out of proportion to a reality danger. She had managed her real fear through repression, projection and displacement. She used avoidance of the activity (stopped jogging, suppressed her anger in her relationship) to manage the enormous internal anxiety she felt. She developed a symptom (fear of jogging and her health, and fear of hurting the man to whom she was committed) in order to avoid the real object of her anxiety (fear of abandonment, fear of the traumatic incident and fear that her anger had killed her brother).

One individual described his feelings during an anxiety attack to Rollo May: "It's like fighting something in the dark when you don't know what it is." And when friends attempted to tell him how to conquer his fears, he responded, "They are like people calling to a drowning man to swim, when they don't know that under the water his hands and feet are tied." (Rollo May, 1979).

Joe

Joe, a gentleman with whom I was working, was constantly terrified that he was going to die. The fear frequently interfered with pleasurable times. He would become almost paralyzed by panic whenever he would catch himself feeling any sense of well-being or joy. Joe's panic blocked a sense of personal freedom. He also could not allow himself any expression of anger in his relationships. After some time in therapy, he related the following incidents from his early childhood.

"I remember being about five or six. My mother asked me to take a watermelon out to our compost heap. She told me not to eat any, just take it out. When I placed it on the heap, it cracked open so I ate some of the center out. When I got back to the house my mother said, 'I hope you didn't eat any. I forgot to tell you that the watermelon was full of poison.' I was terrified. I waited all that day and night to die. I was so sure I was going to die. It was my punishment. How could she do that to me? I was only a kid."

Joe told me of another incident when he was nine or ten. "I was in a bad mood one afternoon. I had to water the garden, and I guess I wanted to do something else, you know. I probably wanted to be with my friends. Anyway, the watering hose got stuck around something. I pulled and pulled. It wouldn't come loose. I was really frustrated and got pretty mad. My mom heard me yelling at the hose. She told me that someday my anger was going to kill somebody. I never let myself get angry after that."

Underlying debilitating anxiety, there is always a conflicted child. In Joe's case two of the conflicts represented were: autonomy and freedom versus the fear of death and expression of anger versus death resulting from his mother's (or his own) rage. The original conflict usually exists between the child's developing identity and extreme limits put on the child by the parent or life situation. In order to protect the developing ego, one side of the conflict is repressed. The symptom, such as Joe's fear of death when expressing personal freedom, protects him from experiencing the overwhelming trauma of the original conflict.

The Conflicted Child

I have seen this "conflicted child" clearly when relating to young adolescents debilitated by school phobia. These young people frequently had many conflict-free periods of school attendance. Abruptly, there is terror of school. When questioning their parents regarding home life at the time of onset of the symptoms, I was frequently told that one or the other parent was critically ill. In some cases, the parents were considering divorce. The children in these cases, for various reasons, felt the dependency needs of the parent, usually the mother. The underlying conflict frequently was the child's developing autonomy versus the loss of a parent due to perceived illness, divorce or emotional instability. These children felt responsible for the parent's well-being.

One 12-year-old boy, who had been working with me for some time, painfully allowed himself to experience the underlying conflict.

"I'm all my mother has. Don't you understand? Since my dad left, I'm the only one she can depend on. She sleeps all the time. I hear her crying at night. One night I heard her on the phone with him, telling him that if it wasn't for me, she couldn't live. If I leave her, too, I mean, if I go to school, I'll probably come home one day and . . . and find her dead. I'm all she has."

A variety of phobic reactions, including school phobia, are frequently rooted in separation anxiety. The onset of symptoms occurring after a threatening situation or extreme frustration experienced by the mother that increases her dependency needs on her child may cause the child to perceive any separation from her, such as going to school, as a traumatic experience.

I have worked with many adult children of survivors of World War I, World War II, Vietnam or the Holocaust who experience debilitating panic attacks. Many of these individuals as children felt extreme responsibility for their parents' lives. They also had repressed, early in childhood, many of their own needs and emotions because of the feeling that they had no right to anger, frustration, normal needs or sadness. At some level they felt they could never presume to suffer as much as their parents had. Many had heard debilitating stories of their parents' survival experiences at early ages and had extreme ambivalence regarding their attachment to their parents. This was frequently represented in the conflict underlying their panic attacks (such as fear of someone breaking into their house and injuring or killing them).

This panic often led to compulsively locking doors and windows over and over again, then staying awake night after night in terror. The underlying conflict might be seen as the need to protect the parent versus rage at the parent's dependency, or guilt over their own survival versus a wish that the parent would die. The underlying repressed rage becomes protected by a symptom that can be focused on and externally controlled (for instance, locking the doors and windows, then checking them repeatedly).

The panic of the adult offers us a window to the frightened child inside. Unfortunately that child is often not seen because it is the symptoms that are most readily in focus. Medications may relieve the heart palpitations, hyperventilation, chest pains and lessen the panic. It is a bit like rubbing a cooling ointment on an infected wound. It may relieve the pain temporarily. Techniques, such as progressive desensitization, may allow the individual relief of the "symptom in focus."

For example, with progressive relaxation and gradual exposure to jogging in incremental steps, Grace may be able to jog again. She may, however, without intervention to the internal child, begin to suffer from stomach pains or night terrors. The skin might heal under the ointment, but the infection may then be forced under the skin and erupt in another location. Treating the symptom may relieve the current distress, but unless the underlying traumas and conflicts are resolved, healthy development will still be blocked.

Many years ago I heard from a peer the story of a woman who had spent her life in a state hospital. Times had changed in the mental health field with the realization that it was more effective to work with patients based in the community rather than keeping them in institutions. The woman expressed excitement at finally leaving the hospital, but her social workers were having difficulty placing her. She was terrified of snakes and could not be convinced that her new location, a rural area, would be free of snakes. Finally, a mobile home was found that was set high off the ground where no snakes could enter. Appearing excited while she made preparations to leave, the woman suddenly became terrified of dogs that might be in the area.

A full year was spent working with the woman to overcome her fear of dogs. Her counselors stayed with her through increased exposure to the dogs in the new neighborhood and also taught her about other animals. She finally made friends with the neighborhood pets. Only days before her scheduled release from the hospital she became ill, then paralyzed from the waist down. No medical cause was found for the sudden paralysis.

If someone had talked to the frightened child inside the woman, the child might have said, "I'm anxious to leave home, but I'm so afraid. If I let you know how afraid I am, I will lose you. I've wanted to leave here all my life. I can't face how dependent and terrified I am. I want to please you so you'll stay with me. I'm enraged at you for rejecting me. I am proud because you have faith in me. I am terrified because I know I can't do what you expect of me. Inside these walls, I am a prisoner. Outside these walls I face emotional starvation and death. I want to grow up. I want to be dependent forever. If I'm not dependent, I will lose you forever. If I remain dependent, I will lose me."

Like the woman in the story, panic always has as its base an underlying struggle that becomes resolved by rendering mute one half of the struggle (repression). Most individuals who suffer from extreme panic in their life often appear at other times, like Grace, as fearless. They have almost become afraid of fear, and the panic they experience frequently is a source of incredible pain. They often feel deep shame as well at allowing the frightened child a voice. Many people who seem surrounded by accomplishments and lots of friends tell me of their internal feelings of isolation and intense loneliness all their lives.

> "Repression sets up inner contradictions within the personality, thus making for a shaky psychological equilibrium, which is bound to be continually threatened in the course of everyday life . . . because of the repression, the individual is less able to distinguish and fight against real dangers as they occur. For example, the person who represses a good deal of aggression and hostility may at the same time assume a compliant and passive attitude toward others, which in turn increases the likelihood that he will be exploited by other people, which in turn gives him more aggression and hostility to repress. Finally, repression increases the individual's feeling of helplessness in that it involves a curtailing of his own autonomy, an inner retrenchment and shelving of his own power."

> May, 1979

Panic attacks involve a relationship between the frightened child and an adult person who the child depended on for security and self-esteem. The focus in reality of the panic is an effort to preserve that relationship and the child's resulting identity and positive sense of self.

Panic attacks can be terrifying. Many individuals who experience symptoms of panic attacks, such as changes in heart rate, profuse sweating and shortness of breath, believe they are in the clutches of impending death. Of those who experience disorientation, confusion and numbness, many fear they are losing control or are "going crazy." The fear of having a panic attack frequently brings on the next one, creating a never-ending spiral of terror and pain.

In order to break this cycle of panic it is helpful to offer the internal frightened child a "cognitive life-raft." Validating the child is the first necessary step in walking back through the trauma in order to achieve emotional mastery. Questions to ask to reach that child might be:

"What do you fear?"

"How does that make you feel?"

"Is the feeling familiar?"

"How old do you feel during a panic attack?"

"What choices are available to you in that situation?"

"What is the worst possible thing that could happen to you as a result of that situation?"

"Imagine yourself taking charge if the worst did happen."

"How does it feel to have power in that situation?"

"How would your life be without the terror you are experiencing?"

These questions frequently start the process of offering a supportive hand to that child. They increase the internal child's sense of safety. They also help to create the sense that the attack can be survived, thereby decreasing the tendency to fight panic with panic.

Asking how life would be without the terror aids in identifying the "wishes" hidden in the "fears."

Grace expressed her greatest fear was that she would die. However, as a child, part of her believed she should have died. When asked how her life would be without the panic attacks, Grace replied "I'd be happier, more successful and finally live in peace." An unconscious "wish" she had deeply repressed was that she die in place of her brother. Her internal child held to the belief that she must be punished and remain unhappy because she had survived.

Many of us, inadvertently, block the attempts of the child in us or in others toward self-preservation. We ignore the child's cries, render the child mute or treat the child with contempt. If we can hear the child's desperation, fears, needs or rage through the panic, we will begin to see the frightened child through a hazy window. It is then that we can offer the child a hand in her attempts at autonomy and freedom.

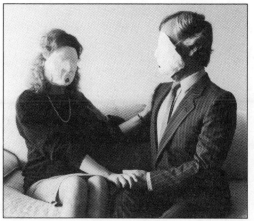

S. A. Harris

FOUR

Relationships:
Attempts At Mastery

". . . I was not comfortable with anyone who was not disapproving of me. No matter how ardently I strove to attain their impossibly high standards for me, I could never do anything entirely right, and so I grew accustomed to that climate of inevitable failure. I hated my mother, so I got back at her by giving my wife her role. In Sallie, I had formed the woman who would be a subtle, more cunning version of my own mother. Like my mother, my wife had come to feel slightly ashamed of and disappointed in me. The configuration and tenor of my weakness would define the fury of their resurrection; my failure would frame their strength, blossoming and deliverance.

"Though I hated my father, I expressed that hatred eloquently by imitating his life, by becoming more and

89

more ineffectual daily, by ratifying all the cheerless prophecies my mother made for both my father and me. I thought I had succeeded in not becoming a violent man, but even that belief collapsed. My violence was subterranean, unbeheld. It was my silence, my long withdrawals, that I had turned into dangerous things. My viciousness manifested itself in the terrible winter of blue eyes. My wounded stare could bring an ice age into the sunniest, balmiest afternoon. I was about to be 37 years old, and with some aptitude and a little natural ability, I had figured out how to live a perfectly meaningless life, but one that could imperceptibly and inevitably destroy the lives of those around me."

from *THE PRINCE OF TIDES* by Pat Conroy

Subway Couple

A number of years ago I was waiting for a subway during rush hour. I did not realize at first that the two individuals standing next to me in the crowded station were partners. They had not spoken, and each stared straight ahead for some time. Then they spoke, seemingly carrying on a conversation that had begun earlier.

"I told you I was sorry. What do you want me to do?"

Silence.

"I didn't forget on purpose, for God's sake. Can't we forget it?"

Silence.

"Look, I'll pick it up tomorrow. Okay? I'm sorry."

"Forget it. I'll pick it up myself. You never forget on purpose. It's like I spend my life talking to a wall. You never remember the things I ask you to do. I might as well be living by myself."

"I do listen to you. Why do you make such a big deal out of everything anyway? Can't we discuss this when we get home? It's not the end of the world! I said I'll get it tomorrow."

"That's what you always say. I'm tired of it. I might as well be invisible. Nothing I feel or need matters in the least to you. It never has."

Silence.

The fight continued inside the crowded subway. The emotions grew more intense with each exchange. Neither seemed interested in resolution. It was as if their lives were at stake. The other passengers seemed to get more tense with them. One little girl stared at them and another began acting up. A man in the seat in front of them snapped his evening paper many times, apparently irritated at being forced to listen. The longer they spoke, the more crowded the car seemed to become. I could almost feel the presence of their families standing next to them. Perhaps there was a parent who never listened, another who nagged.

I thought of the couple I had seen in my office at the end of the day and the child I had observed in play therapy that morning. The couple had a similar argument, and like the pair in the subway, what was being spoken about had little to do with the real conflict between them.

Tom and Sally

Tom: I never feel like I'm enough for you. You always want me to be someone I'm not.

Sally: It has nothing to do with being enough, Tom. I would just like you, for once, to care about my feelings.

Tom: I do care about your feelings, damn it. What does what I wear to dinner have to do with your feelings?

Sally: Respect, that's what. You always embarrass me and you don't care. You never care about me. What I feel doesn't matter.

Middelton-Moz: Sally, who else could you be talking to right now? Who's standing next to Tom?

Sally: Well, maybe my mother. She always embarrassed me when she came to school. She wasn't like the other parents. God, I feel so guilty saying that. She couldn't help it. She was from the old country and we were poor.

Middelton-Moz: Did you ever talk to her about your feelings?

Sally: Not really. I couldn't. She couldn't help it. I felt so awful even feeling that way. She and Papa worked hard and their lives were so painful before they came here. How could I have been so petty. I don't know. God, I remember once in junior high when I was in a school play. I didn't want Mama and Papa to come. They didn't look or talk like the other kids' parents and at that time I was trying so hard to fit in. I asked them not to come and told them I would be nervous if they were in the audience. I can still see the pain in Mama's eyes. She had suffered enough. I can't believe I was so selfish. (Sally began to cry and Tom comforted her.)

Later in the session:

Middelton-Moz: Tom, a while ago when you and Sally were arguing, who might have been standing by her? Who else might you have been talking to?

Tom: Probably my mom, too. Also, I think I might have wanted my dad to hear me. He never stood up to her. She controlled both of us. She picked out my clothes when I was in high school. It was like Dad and I were never quite right.

At the end of the session Tom and Sally were comforting each other instead of attacking and blaming. I reminded them that those kids who were in such pain probably would have liked each other.

Sally, the oldest child of immigrant parents, had been in the position as a child of split loyalties. She was her parents' "ambassador" to the new world. It had been her job to teach them the language and be their buffer. They had little idea of her struggles. Because she was so aware of their pain (they had lived through the war in Europe and had suffered great losses in immigration), she found it necessary to repress her needs and feelings as a child. She had heard and seen their suffering repeatedly and been reminded constantly of how hard they worked. She felt her own pain and needs were undeserved, selfish and meaningless. As a child, she remembered being taught that she could never presume to suffer as they had suffered. She learned to feel guilty for her happiness and successes. Success meant leaving them behind.

Sally had spent her entire life trying to fit in. She had copied others' manners in restaurants, studied styles of dress in magazines and on store mannequins. When Tom dressed differently from those around them, it brought up in her the pain of "childhood visibility," of feeling "different." She felt the anger that she had repressed toward her parents for needing to be so responsible for herself and them. It also brought up the anger toward the broader majority culture that had caused her to feel so uncomfortable outside her home.

When Sally nagged and complained about Tom's dress, it set off in him the rage he felt toward his overly controlling, overly protective mother and passive father. He felt the old pain of "never being enough for his mother." His way of attempting to keep his identity as a child was to covertly rebel and become "mother deaf." He was now using the same protectiveness with Sally. In addition to attempts to protect his identity, he was also trying to make up for his father's passiveness.

Both Sally and Tom were working out old traumas in their new marriage. They had given each other the faces of early attachment figures. It was difficult with this family reunion so present in every discussion to communicate with each other or reach any successful resolution of differences. Painful childhood struggles for identity and nurturing cannot find resolution in present-day intimate relationships. The strength of Sally's and Tom's emotions in their conflicts, and their resistance in reaching compromise, indicated that they were attempting to resolve old painful traumas in a new relationship.

Lucas

Earlier that morning I had watched four-year-old Lucas in the playroom. He had placed the daddy doll with his back toward the scene that was being played out. The little boy doll was hitting the mama doll as Lucas carefully guided its movements.

"Bad mama. Bad mama. You lef' me. Bad mama."

Lucas' mother stood with me behind the two-way mirror, tears sliding down her face. "It hurts to know how much pain he's been in, but boy, am I glad he's getting it out. He must have felt so alone. It really makes me understand how little children understand, yet we expect them to."

Lucas had been in an automobile accident with his mother several months before. She had been badly hurt but Lucas had only been slightly bruised. While his mother had been taken into surgery immediately, Lucas had waited in the emergency room for his dad. She had been in the hospital for five weeks. Since his mother was a single parent, Lucas had stayed with his dad and stepmother while his mom was recuperating in the hospital, then later at home. Lucas had been terrified to ride in cars since the accident.

His parents had divorced before his first birthday and his father had immediately married the woman to whom he had been previously engaged. Lucas' mother seemed to have successfully worked through a good deal of bitterness.

"It wasn't anybody's fault. I see that now. We were married only six months after he had broken his engagement to Ruth and he had been with her almost seven years. I should have known better than to marry him so soon, but I was used to being second choice in my family. My sister was always the favored one. Counseling has helped. I was in a lot of pain for a while. I realize now it was old pain, not just the pain of the divorce. I think Bob still feels guilty, though. Ruth tries to be pleasant, but I think she sometimes resents Lucas and me. She can't have children of her own."

Bob's guilt was apparent. When Lucas had stayed with him and his wife, he had found it difficult to talk to his son about the accident.

"I felt so bad, so responsible. If I hadn't left them, hadn't been so selfish, it never would have happened. I couldn't talk to Ruth either. It was like I resented her for my own choices. I've always felt resentful toward my mother, too. My dad left when I was two and I always felt responsible for her, guilty and responsible. I could never make her happy."

A week or so after the accident Lucas had said to his father, "We're mad at Mommy, aren't we? She left both of us."

After Lucas had received a verbal scolding for his feelings, he became super-good, super-helpful. However, he began wetting his bed again and having night terrors. He froze whenever he was put in his car seat. Refusal to ride in the car, however, did not occur until he was back with his mother. The night terrors continued, as did his bed-wetting. His mother felt it was wise to bring him in for counseling.

Lucas was seen in play therapy for several weeks while his parents and stepmother were in family counseling. They were also allowed to observe Lucas in the playroom as he worked through the traumatic events surrounding the accident. Shortly after he began expressing his fears and rage in the playroom, his bed-wetting and night terrors ceased. After some time he mastered the trauma of the accident.

Lucas zoomed two cars down his make-believe highway. When one car was about to hit the other, he stopped. He walked over to the toy chest, selected a huge plastic bulldozer from the pile of toys and returned to the unfolding drama. He re-enacted the scene. This time though, when the red car was about to crash into the blue car (his mother's car had been blue), he grabbed the bulldozer and shoved the red car off the road. He sat for a few minutes, observing the scene with an expression of power on his face, then did it all over again. He glanced up at the play therapist, "The red car is bad. It hurt my mommy and me, but it's not goin' to anymore."

Lucas's parents looked on with amazement. Bob spoke, "It's amazing, isn't it. I've watched him here each week relive the days he spent with me, his anger at his mom, me, Ruth and now the accident. It's like he's reliving every torment in his life. In the playroom, though, he has the control. I wonder what would have happened if we could have had that opportunity years ago in our own childhoods?"

Lucas' mother glanced at him, "Maybe we could have gone through all the pain in the playroom. We had to act it out in adult life. It's like we did it with each other instead of the dolls Lucas has acted out with."

"Only Lucas gets to move them the way he wants to. He gets to resolve it. With us, it only seems to get worse. We felt all the pain, guilt and anger and it still wasn't resolved. We didn't know what we were doing," Bob said reflectively.

"Right," Ruth added, "our dolls were real people. We didn't get to control them. God knows we tried." Ruth laughed and was joined by the others.

Bob and Ruth were correct. The pain, unmet needs and unresolved traumas of childhood and pain from past generations reappear as themes in dysfunctional and oftentimes repetitive relationships. What Lucas acted out in the playroom, Bob, Ruth and Lucas' mom acted out in their relationships. They, too, were attempting resolution of painful, anxious attachments with parental figures and unresolved traumas in present and past generations.

Sally and Tom were the partners on the subway attempting resolution as well. Their attempts, however, were unconscious. There was no one there to validate the events or their feelings, aid them in resolution or allow them the space and time to walk back through their pain with guidance.

Perhaps without guidance from his mother, Lucas too would have continued his father's and grandfather's painful legacy of detachment and guilt, or felt and acted out his mother's pain of always feeling like "somebody's second choice." In his own future committed relationships, he may have fought with his partner over driving the car and never known that underneath this conflict was a fear of abandonment. We can sometimes see in our new family "playroom," the scenes, dramas and painful events that never could be talked about or be expressed in our childhoods or during the growing-up years of our parents and grandparents.

Conscious Decisions, Unconscious Choices

Many years ago I worked with a woman who had successively married seven alcoholic men. She told me that she "never knew any of them drank before I married them." At about the same time, I worked with a man who had been married four times and each woman had extramarital affairs shortly after he married her. He said, "Each woman was so committed to me, to the marriage, before we wed. How did it happen over and over again in the same way?" Another woman found out information about her husband only after their marriage vows that caused her to keep secrets from her friends and to feel extreme shame. The same thing happened in her second marriage. Still another woman I was seeing had been in four relationships with suicidal partners.

The first woman's father and grandfather had been alcoholic. She had made a promise to herself in childhood never to live as her mother and grandmother had. The man whose wives had affairs had an extremely enmeshed relationship with his mother until she deserted the family when he was six. The woman who felt shame in her marriages felt ashamed of her parents' behavior and the state of her home throughout childhood. She led two lives, never bringing anyone home. The woman with four suicidal partners had a mother and two favorite aunts commit suicide before she was 18.

In doing genogram (family mapping) work with couples over the years, I have seen consistent, repetitive themes emerge and re-emerge in interactions and conflicts that had begun in earlier generations. Themes of distance, conflict, enmeshment, alcoholism, abuse, affairs, divorce, depression, financial instability, inability to bond, suicidal ideation, etc., seemed to show themselves in generation after generation. One might ask, as one woman did, "How can this happen? How could I have known? It wasn't like that between us before commitment."

We tend to seek out when choosing a partner, what is familiar in much the same way that someone from another country might seek out others with the same customs, language and values. We learned how to survive and adapt in dysfunctional families through use of particular defenses, nonverbal communication, cues, mannerisms and adaptive behaviors.

In our families of origin, we develop many beliefs about ourselves in relation to each other and the world. We are allowed expression of some emotions and not others. We seek out partners who allow us to "be at home" and continue these beliefs and expressions on the one hand, while we continue to attempt resolution for the once-discarded child.

Tom, for instance, knew how to behave when someone nagged. Nagging fit with the belief he had about himself and the world. Yet he had tremendous anger regarding a childhood where he felt overly controlled. It would have been far more difficult and uncomfortable to be with someone who accepted him as he was.

Sally was used to feeling visible, embarrassed and responsible. Her relationship with Tom allowed her to continue those familiar feelings and resulting defenses, yet she felt tremendous unresolved pain and anger in the relationship for those same feelings. For each, the relationship was familiar. Each had chosen unconsciously in their partners, the characteristics necessary for continued self-defense and, at the same time, as the backdrop necessary for resolution of old pain and anger that had never been resolved.

Although frequently viewed by ourselves and others as unhealthy, the compulsion to repeat old traumas in order to attempt to work them through might well be viewed as a consistent striving toward resolution and health.

Liz and Mark

Liz expressed her first impression of Mark, her husband, this way: "He was standing on a chair putting in a light bulb. He looked so gentle, so helpless in many ways. He wasn't tough and macho like the other men I had seen in college. He looked so vulnerable somehow." Yet it was that same "vulnerability" that attracted her, which became the "dependency" she hated and had fought so desperately against in their marriage. Later in couples' therapy, she shared a fantasy that she believed she had also had early in their courtship.

"My dad was alcoholic. He was also kinder and gentler than my mother was. I hated the way she treated him. My dad died of alcoholism when I was in my teens. I guess I always thought he would have lived if my mother had been kinder to him. I think I was afraid of becoming like my mother somehow, so I always put Mark's feelings first and made excuses for him. But I was tired of being hurt and disappointed. I think I thought I could save Mark if I took care of him. I could help him grow up and take care of me in the way my father never could. I guess I've never accepted my anger at Dad before now either."

Mark was attracted to Liz for different reasons. "She was so stable and strong. I thought I could lean on her in ways I never could my mother. Mother was really crazy, erratic. Liz was the perfect mom. She accepted me and was understanding of my faults. After we were married, though, I felt her resentment. Her 'understanding' made me feel worse about myself. My mother yelled at me but never followed through on any limits. Liz was calm, but resented it somehow and never accepted me as a man. I guess I realized that she didn't respect me any more than Mom did and I didn't respect myself. Neither Mom nor Liz expected me to be responsible. I was still in my same role. I hated her and myself, just like I had with Mom."

Liz had promised herself that she would never be like her mother. Her choice in partner and attitude about herself, however, was similar. She became like the flip side of her mother, just as she had always felt growing up. Liz also learned while doing family research for her genogram, that her grandmother had been a passive sweet caretaker. Liz's mother's reaction to her mother's passive lack of assertion was to become pushy, bossy and "always angry." The choice of "dependent" men had not changed. Neither had the counterdependence of the women in her family for three generations.

It is almost as if an unconscious contract is signed along with the marriage contract or commitment agreement. These nonverbal unconscious agreements, however, frequently carry more weight in reconstructing our own legacies. Some might read:

"I promise that I will keep the distance and you can fight it."

"I'll promise to avoid intimacy if you will."

"I'll be dependent and you can take care of me."

"I'll keep up a wall and you can try to fight through it."

"I'll disappoint you and you can punish me."

"We will both hold each other accountable for keeping up an image."

"I'll be the sick one. You can be the healthy one."

"I'll get all my needs met and feel guilty and you can get none of yours met and feel superior."

"We will both agree to allow each other the same self-concept and defenses we had growing up and at the same time aid each other in recreating the old traumas and hurts to fight through."

Maggie Scarf (1987) said it well,

"It is in marriage that we resurrect not only the intensity of our first attachment feelings, but the miseries of old frustrations and repressed hatreds as well. And what is so frequently sought in a mate — and then fought out with that mate — is some unresolved dilemma about a parent."

Play It Again, Sam

Margaret and Ellen

Margaret sat as far in the corner of the couch as she possibly could without going over the edge. Her arms were tightly folded in front of her, as if in protection. Ellen sat on the other side of the couch, tense, but her voice appeared level. Her legs were crossed and the top one was moving up and down as she spoke, "Come on, Margaret, I know you're angry. Why don't you talk about it? That's what we're here for, you know."

"I am not angry! Why do you always tell me what I think?"

Ellen: I can tell you're angry. You haven't talked to me all morning. Come on. What did I do wrong this time?

Margaret: Nothing. Can't a person just have a bad mood without it being a federal case?

Middelton-Moz: Ellen, are you angry?

Ellen: No, she is.

Middelton-Moz: Can you tell me what your foot is saying?

(Ellen looked at her foot wildly rocking up and down, laughed, then began to cry. Margaret unfolded her arms and turned toward Ellen. After a few minutes had passed, Ellen spoke.)

Ellen: I don't know. I'm sick of trying to figure it out all by myself, I guess. Maybe I am a little frustrated.

Middelton-Moz: Why do you . . . Why do you try to figure it out all by yourself?

Ellen: Because she won't ever tell me what she's feeling.

Middelton-Moz: And? What happens if she's feeling something and doesn't tell you?

Ellen: (Looks confused, stares off into space for some time, then starts to cry again) It makes me anxious, scares me. I don't know why. I have no reason to be afraid of Margaret, she's never hurt me.

Middelton-Moz: Was there anyone in your life who you had cause to fear when they were quiet?

Ellen: No. Nobody ever hurt me. My mom was nice but she wasn't there much. She worked a lot. My dad was always quiet and kept to himself until . . . (She began to cry again.) . . . until he killed himself. God, I never knew how bad he felt. I never really knew him.

Middelton-Moz: Ellen, can you tell Margaret how much it frightens you when she goes into a "bad mood?"

(Ellen talked to Margaret about her feelings as a child when her dad would "go away." She said she felt badly about herself and even when she was little, it had made her angry. After his suicide, she said, she had felt responsible for never realizing what he was feeling. Ellen cried while Margaret held her and reassured her that she was not considering suicide and never had. Then towards the end of the session . . .)

Middelton-Moz: Margaret, at the beginning of the session it seemed that if you could have seated yourself in mid-air, you would have moved right off the couch. What were you saying with your body?

(Both Margaret and Ellen laughed at the visual image of Margaret sitting in mid-air.)

Margaret: I was trying to get away, I guess. Sometimes, Ellen, when you try to get inside my head, it makes me uncomfortable. I feel like I have nothing of my own, not even my own thoughts.

In sessions following this, both women talked more about their growing-up years. Ellen's father and mother had very little communication. Margaret, an only child, felt totally engulfed by her mother. She said her mother had opened her mail, listened in on her phone conversations, and "always made a big deal out of everything." The only way she could protect herself from losing her identity, Margaret said, was to say nothing, feel nothing and be out of the house as much as possible.

Margaret's alone time and distance had been a repetitive theme in arguments between her and Ellen. Ellen's mindreading and constant therapizing had also been an issue between them. As time went on, Ellen was able to see that the anger she had accused Margaret of feeling was really her own. She had repressed anger since her father's death and had projected it onto others in relationships. The dependency that Margaret feared from Ellen became more understandable to her as Ellen moved away. Her fear was really the wish that her own unmet dependency needs could be filled by another. Because Margaret's mother had been so engulfing, dependency had been dangerous to her growing identity. She had, therefore, repressed her needs and projected them onto the significant others.

Both Margaret and Ellen had served as mirrors for the other's disowned and discarded child. They had also served as old attachment figures for each other in an attempt to work out childhood trauma. As painful memories were stimulated and restimulated in therapy through guidance in repetitive conflict resolution, Margaret and Ellen were able to see each other as the individuals they truly were. Their real relationship was allowed to begin and grow.

Many couples become involved in a repetitive dance. Without guidance, couples find it difficult to change the steps enough so that the dance allows for spontaneous communication. The background music, like the sound of a phonograph needle stuck in the same groove, guides their steps endlessly in the same compulsive unsatisfying pattern. It is the music born out of the pain of traumatic childhoods, set in an album of past unresolved generations. This type of compulsive, repetitive dance in relationships, where compromises, risks of vulnerability, respect for separate selves and exploration of feelings is rarely seen, is evidence that a couple is re-enacting past experiences rather than living in the current relationship. The music requires rigidity in movement, proof of a love that will heal past wounds and fill empty spaces, requiring total involvement in the dance and preoccupation with the dance partner. The trophies given for this marathon are limited. Control is the prize for forsaking love, and love is awarded for giving up all control. Self-power and love, co-existing against the spontaneous backdrop of personal freedom, are never in the running for the strict judges of the past that sponsor this dance.

Marionettes

by J. Danielsen

How like marionettes we are, one to another
When, with tangled strings we move each other
Uncertain of which string goes where.
So twisted up . . . it's hard to care.

Should we learn a string or two
Pensively, we begin anew
Sorting through the tangled mess
In search of nothing . . . more or less.

I know this string, it invokes surprise.
Pull this one and someone cries.
This one I have never seen.
(Or taken note of it . . . I mean.)
This one, perhaps I know about, but . . .
Dare I touch it if there is any doubt?

Releasing the strings at hand we find
Joy, through movements of a kind
That radiate from our common mind
Through golden strings that love entwined.

AND BABY MAKES . . . A CROWD?

Judy and Ralph and Joan . . . and Peter

Judy was late for the school bus almost every morning. Most of the time the bus came and went without her. Her mother would usually drive her to school. Judy's parents had purchased an assortment of alarm clocks, some with music, some with beeps. All the alarms would sound in unison at 7:00 in the morning. Judy would reach over and methodically turn each one off, waiting for her mother's angry footsteps to come up the stairs at 7:15 yelling, "Come on, Judy, for God's sake, get up!" Her mother would then rush back down the stairs to finish preparing breakfast. Judy's father would come into her room at about 7:25, after her mother had complained to him about Judy's behavior. He would warn her that if she did not get up, "There will be hell to pay." At this point Judy would have only 20 minutes to catch the bus.

While still in bed, Judy would hear her parents fighting about her behavior. Her mother would protest that her father's threats had been too harsh. Ten minutes later her mother would again climb the stairs and urge Judy to get up. Judy would then get up and slowly dress for school while continuing to listen to her parents fight. Usually she would also be warned that if she did not move faster, she would have to walk. Sometimes she would hear her younger brother trying to distract the parents' argument. His attempts would be ignored.

Judy would dawdle over breakfast, listening to a long lecture from her dad. She knew she would not have to walk to school. Her mother would generally apologize for her dad's lectures while driving her to the front door of the school just as the bell rang. The chaos would repeat itself that night over her homework and then usually again the following morning. (Middelton-Moz, 1985).

Joan and Ralph, Judy's parents, were a sincere, concerned couple in their mid 30s. They were highly committed to being good parents and were puzzled by the difficulties they were having with Judy. They both wanted their children to have the good homelife neither of them had had. Each felt insecure in the role of parent. They alternately blamed each other and themselves for somehow blowing it with Judy, although they felt proud of their parenting of Peter, Judy's younger brother.

Peter was a quiet six-year-old, who was doing extremely well in school, always waited patiently for the bus to arrive each morning and did his chores without being told. Sometimes, however, Ralph would get frustrated with Peter's goodness.

"He'll let Judy get away with anything. He always shares with her and she rarely reciprocates. It makes me mad at him sometimes."

Neither realized that they often ignored Peter's emotional need for nurturing in much the same way their childhood needs had been ignored.

Both Ralph and Joan came from highly dysfunctional families. Each had one parent who was alcoholic (Judy's mother and Ralph's father), and one continually frustrated parent who functioned in a caretaking role for the alcoholic spouse. Both were the eldest children in their families. Ralph's role in his family was that of constant pleaser while Joan had been the domestic manager responsible for running the house. Her mother frequently would not get up in the morning and it would be Joan's job to get herself and her siblings off to school. In Ralph's case, it had been his father who often would not get up in the morning. Ralph had memories of constantly trying to make his mother feel better so there would not be any fights.

Even though Joan and Ralph felt very proud of never becoming alcoholics themselves, they were astonished to realize that the mornings in their new family felt similar to their growing-up years.

"You're right. It does feel the same," Ralph replied with amazement. "But how is that possible? Neither Joan nor I have ever been drinkers. We've tried so hard to make it different. We've tried to be such responsible parents. We talk to our kids and hear them out. I think we've read every child-rearing book the library has to offer."

Like many parents that grew up in dysfunctional families, Ralph's and Joan's childhood issues had reappeared in their new family. Just as commitment in relationships stimulate early traumas of attachment, the birth of children frequently signal painful memories of our own childhoods. With each passing stage of our children's development, memories and emotions of that stage are revived inside us.

Sometimes we have difficulty setting limits and following through for our children in an attempt to reparent ourselves. Their sadness becomes our sadness, their failures our failures. Or perhaps we become angry and enraged at the same traits in our children that have caused us pain inside ourselves. Sometimes, in an effort to be the reverse of our parents, we become a "buddy" to our children, rather than a parent. In some families children become the focus of the resentment the parent felt for their parents.

> "In fact, some young parents suffer, it seems, from the retardation of the ability to develop this stage. The reasons are often to be found in early childhood impressions."
>
> Erikson, 1963

Early emotional neglect of one's children can often be found in a type of self-focus based on a too strenuously self-made personality. (Erikson, 1963).

Joan and Ralph re-experienced the ambivalent feelings each felt at age nine through the ritual morning struggle with nine-year-old Judy. Joan grew up angry towards her hungover, sleeping mother. She felt responsible for her drinking and feelings in much the same way she felt ambivalent toward Judy's behavior. When Joan would attempt to follow through on limits with Judy, such as "You'll have to walk to school," Judy's tears would bring back her own childhood frustration and pain. She would reparent her internal child by withdrawing the limit. When Ralph would show anger at Judy, Joan would defend her in much the same way she protected her mother from her father's anger.

Ralph had a similar scenario. He was angry at his sleeping father, yet protective of him, attempting, as a child, to save his male model and his own self-esteem. He fluctuated between feeling responsible for his mother's feelings, in the way his father was not, and blaming his mother for his father's drinking (in much the same way he blamed Joan for Judy's behavior).

Both adults fluctuated in their feelings toward Peter, their "good" son. Sometimes they ignored him, as they had been ignored as children. Other times Joan felt sorry for him, like she had for herself. Ralph on occasion was angry at Peter's passiveness, wishing he would fight back in a way that Ralph never had.

As had been the case in the families of origin, Ralph and Joan also repeated the pattern of triangles, black-and-white thinking and looped communication in their new family. They rarely spent time together without the kids or without arguing about the kids. Joan would align with Ralph against Judy, then with Judy against Ralph. They would communicate with each other about the children's behavior: with Peter about Judy, with Judy about Peter, or with either of the children about the other parent. Are you confused with all these loops? So were they. Joan and Ralph rarely directly communicated feelings with the person with whom they had the conflict or concern. Furthermore, when Joan or Ralph would defend Judy, it would frequently stimulate the early pain and rage of parental abandonment in the other.

The forming of triangles in family relationships occurs for many reasons:

1. It was the pattern of communication taught in each spouse's family of origin.
2. Having someone in the middle offers a protection against feared rejection or engulfment in intimate relationships.
3. Triangular interactions supply the familiarity of the original dysfunctional family.
4. Establishing family triangles unconsciously allows for a multitude of new roles for attempted resolution of childhood trauma.

5. "Good" versus "bad" splits in families unconsciously allow ways to project disowned characteristics in the self onto others and also punish those feelings in the self. (For example, the parent who is terrified of his anger, frequently has a child who they cannot control. The punishment of that child is left to the other parent.)

6. Family realignment and triangular communication unconsciously allows for adult individuals, who have never completed their own emotional development because of their own childhood trauma, to avoid the mature role as spouse or parent for which they are unequipped. (This is true of multigenerational incest in families. One parent may opt out of the intimate relationship with her partner and the parenting role with the child. Both parents are seeking the unconditional love and nurturing they never received. One parent may try to get her needs for acceptance, nurturing and approval met outside the home, while the other inappropriately aligns with the child against the other parent. The realigned relationship that starts out as an inappropriate need for nurturing, acceptance and fulfillment from a child is covertly sexually abusive as the child becomes the parent's mate. Sometimes overt sexual abuse occurs as the inappropriate alignment increases and the parent seeks total new fulfillment from the child. Secrets increase the power of the parent/child enmeshment. Without intervention, the abused child never learns the difference between nurturing and sexuality, and frequently is part of a newly created triangle in their newly established family.)

7. Unconscious triangular relationships allow the couple to project onto their children all the problems and unresolved conflicts in their marriage as were frequently projected onto each of them by their parents.

"The couple usually sees themselves in unison; they have no difficulties aside from the ones that they are having with their unmanageable offspring." (Scarf, 1987). This creates the frequently recurring family dynamic of "us against them." This type of couple has created difficulty communicating, building a relationship and connecting without something or someone to fight against together.

As stated so well by Scarf (1987):

> "A three-legged table is, obviously, easier to keep in a balanced state than a two-legged table — or relationship — which is far less stable by nature."

In many cases couples who have each come from traumatic families have never been alone. Many couples choose to live with their families of origin or have friends staying with them from the onset of marriage. Sometimes there are realistic emergencies or financial needs to do so. They may often have children immediately to fill a gap in the relationship. Each additional party that is either present or can be triangulated in the couple's argument ("My friends don't like you, either") offers another person capable of wearing a costume and mask in the ongoing replay of the traumatic past.

Triangular communication offers further familiarity of the past in multigenerational traumatic families. Disappointed in their marriage, adult children of trauma make the same mistakes their parents did. In forming triangles, they can express repressed rage at a spouse and attempt to receive from a child that which cannot be risked from a partner. Those needs that were never supplied in childhood and demanded instead often seek fulfillment inappropriately from the child in the next generation. If one's spouse is psychologically absent, the parent might turn to the child to fill the internal loneliness and feel more fulfilled in terms of self-esteem. (Fossum and Mason). The child, who cannot fill the void left from the past, frequently feels failure in this role and fears both intimacy and the parenting role in his adulthood.

After some time in therapy, Joan and Ralph were able to change their parenting styles with both Judy and Peter. The children responded initially with confusion, no longer knowing their places in the system. Initially, too, more pressure was put on Joan and Ralph in terms of communication in their marriage.

"You know," Ralph said in one session, "it's hard. I realize now that Joan and I had never really been alone before. Oh, there were always good excuses, a friend needing a place to stay, then Joan's sister. It was so hard just getting to know each other. I think that's what all our fights have really been about lately. Here, however, we've learned to keep working it through and with each resolution, we're closer. It's like a pioneering effort, though. Our parents never really related to us or each other and that's sad."

In a later session, Joan discussed her grief, "You know, I realized the way Ralph and I set it up, there was constant chaos, just like there used to be in my own house. I think our whole family was there every morning, like a demanding crowd in the kitchen. This week, after the kids left for school and Ralph was gone to work, I realized the house was really quiet. I had the day off. All of a sudden, I couldn't stand the quiet. I started compulsively cleaning. I began sorting the boxes of clothes in the attic, and I came upon a little pink dress that had been Judy's when she was about one. It said 'I love you mommy' on the attached bib. It had been a present from Ralph. Well, I can't believe it; I started crying and crying. I think I cried most of the day in that quiet house. At first I thought I was crying 'cause Judy was really growing up. Then I realized it was for my own mom, not just the alcoholic mom that died, but the fantasy Mom I never had. Maybe the fantasy grandmother, too." Ralph moved closer and put his arm around Joan, then spoke, "It's amazing what you feel without the crowd keeping you moving all the time! I think I bought that dress because of the fantasy Mom I never had either."

Coming Home

by Nanci Presley-Holley

My inner child's best friend
is coming to visit.
The mother's little girl
is returning home from school.
The adolescent's mirror
is coming back.
The person who I have
the most guilt about.

I finished cleaning her room this morning.
It's been hell you know.
It's taken me six months
To face that reality.
I remember
the daughter who slept there.
The punk rocker who drugged there.
The little girl who wept there.

Her room was like a time machine
and took me to the past.
Proof positive
of my inability to parent,
to provide structure and strength.
To discipline
and define boundaries,
and catch her when she fell.
Hold her in despair,
to keep her safe from others
and from herself.

How could I do it for her,
when I couldn't even do it for myself?

Living Out Or Undoing Family Trauma:
Superglue Or Isolation

Ruth

Ruth curled up in the corner of the couch. It was as if she was trying to disappear. Her eyes were filled with sadness as she spoke.

"It's like I don't have any family left. I mean, I have a wonderful, caring husband and my children are really special, but I have no mother and father, really, and my children have no grandparents. It's almost worse to have them alive and not have them. Knowing they are there and not there is like a constant reminder that I have done everything wrong in their eyes. It's so painful not to be able to communicate with them."

Middelton-Moz: Did it ever occur to you, Ruth, that on some level you have done exactly what they wanted for you?

Ruth: No. I have been rebelling since I was a child in one way or another. I've always been a fighter.

Middelton-Moz: Were you born fighting?

Ruth: Well, no, I guess not. (She looked surprised by my question.)

Middelton-Moz: Tell me again how you have hurt them.

Ruth: Well, I married outside my faith. That's probably the biggest one. They haven't talked to me since. Then before that, I left the family and went to college, then to law school. My parents are really traditional, as I've told you, and a girl wasn't supposed to go away to college like that.

Middelton-Moz: How do you think it was that you did all those things? Do you think you ever received double messages from them?

Ruth: You know, it's odd. (Ruth relaxed her body, straightened her shoulders a bit as she gazed into space and continued.) It's like they were always proud of my grades, and even though they fought me about going to college, they let me go. They just didn't want me to talk with anyone about it. I think in some ways they were happy I graduated and went to law school. I can't explain it. I've never really thought about it before. How is that possible? I mean, the messages were always clear . . . or maybe they weren't. But why?

Middelton-Moz: Sometimes on a deep level, parents want things for their children they could not have. They want them to experience less pain than they experienced. Maybe, in a way, they were trying to undo their pain through you. Is that possible?

Ruth shifted in her chair. She was silent for some time then tears began streaming down her cheeks.

"You know when I first came in, I did that genogram with you and something puzzled me. Not in my head, really, but deep down inside. Now, I know what it was. I looked at my parents' families wiped out in concentration camps. Mostly the little girls and women were dead. Before the camps, there was so much success, so much affluence in the family. But when they came from the old country to the United States, they were so poor. We were poor. I realized that my life now, at least in terms of finances and status, is like the generations before the camps." She paused, "I'm the eldest daughter. Maybe they wanted me to survive. By marrying outside the faith, maybe they wanted my children to survive, too. My God, it's almost like undoing all that death. I was even named for my mother's little sister who died. On some level, maybe they were teaching me how to be a survivor."

Ruth, like so many of the adult children of parents who lived through trauma (disaster, war, concentration camps, family deaths, and poverty), who I have worked with over the years, seemed to be living a life in order to undo the traumas of the past. Yet in some aspects, these children repeat the family legacy of pain. Like her mother and father after the war, Ruth felt alone, grief-stricken and separated from family. During her time in therapy, she was able to remember that she had received clear messages from her parents which led to many of the decisions she had made (unknowingly) in her adult life.

Her parents actually told her very little about their experiences in the camps, but let her know that the girls and women in her family were more frequently killed than were the men and boys. She had somehow learned to believe that it was because the females lacked the skills and abilities that males possessed. Also she received the clear message that the children were killed because they were "Jews." She was verbally scolded for going to college, but nonverbally rewarded. Her parents had named her after her mother's younger sister, who had been killed and told her to name her own children after other relatives who had died. She had been taught that the tough survived. Rarely had she seen any signs of grief in her parents, yet she now found herself acting out much of the pain they had experienced. Although her husband was never accepted into the family, she was and her children were able to have grandparents. Ruth was able to be more accepting of her own choices, allow her parents their ways and feel empathy for her own pain, while accepting her parents as they were.

Parents who have lived through trauma and tragedy frequently had to develop extreme denial in order to survive. There was often no one available with whom they could talk or grieve; the demands of surviving day-to-day life allowed little time for remembering, feeling and working through old pain. Their own unresolved traumas and denial of the emotional pain attached to them frequently created the foundations, unspoken rules and roles in their new families. Their children often ended up experiencing the pain and grief in their own lives that their parents never could allow. Children from traumatic families also may find themselves making conscious decisions based on unconscious motivations that are directly related to the undoing of their parents' painful lives. Frequently these children reach adulthood, establish professional lives and form relationships without an awareness of how they got where they are. They feel empty, depressed and un-fulfilled upon reaching the goals they set. A successful physician likened it to finishing a play.

"It's almost like I've been playing out a drama written by someone else. My focus in life, all my life, has been to get here, to grow up, become a doctor, open a practice and get married. Now I don't know why. I don't remember ever making these decisions and I feel so empty inside."

> "In a system in which specific expectations about each one's role or function pre-exist, the individuation of each member will encounter strong obstacles . . . In fact, the imbalance between the performance requested and the child's emotional immaturity makes his behavior an empty recitation."
>
> Andolfi et al, 1983

In families where parents, and often grandparents, suffer from delayed grief, the major functional defense is denial. In some families, trauma, such as death of a parent or sibling, is never discussed.

In other families, the traumatic events of the past are constantly discussed but the feelings associated with them are denied.

In still other families, traumatic events are discussed, emotions regarding them expressed, but emotions of the children in the family are never allowed. (For instance, the pain of the child is viewed as insignificant to the original trauma, "You can't presume to suffer as I have suffered.") In these families, because of the parents' survival guilt, the children's joy and laughter are frequently met with ridicule or severe punishment. In families where denial is extreme, children feel separated from their parents on the one hand and glued to them on the other.

For instance, a young woman who had been brutally

beaten in a robbery remembered her parents' reaction to her in the hospital.

"I was lying there all bandaged and bruised. It was like they never noticed the pain I was in or what had happened. They just talked on about all that was going on in my brother's and sister's lives. They even started telling jokes. I so wanted their support. I worked up all my courage and started telling them how much pain I was in. They physically turned away, then my mother told me it would be better not to think about it and just concentrate on getting on with my life. I did. I didn't talk about it again until now. I gained 50 pounds shortly after that. It's like I'm not close to my parents at all, yet I'm bound to them."

Other families appear to move almost in unison. If one member feels something, it's expected that they all will. It appears that all are emotionally joined at the hip. Members finish each other's sentences and are criticized if they have a separate mood.

One young man put it this way, "It's like my mother thinks she and I are the same person. I can be really happy about something and if she isn't, I change my mood. My whole family is like that. One day I had just received a promotion at work. My dad had a bad day. I was telling him my news, and he asked me how I could be so happy when he'd had such a lousy day. It's like I'm expected to live their lives."

As is often the case in families of trauma, the woman who had been hurt and wanted caring empathy from her parents, smothered her own children with emotional reactions. Her little boy reported, "I can't tell Mom anything. It's like my hurts make her hurt."

The spouse of the man who felt "joined at the hip" to his family, explained that he constantly had a wall around him. "If I feel anything, he leaves. He's always telling our son to 'act like a man'. Our little boy is only six. It's hard to believe that he comes from such an emotional family."

Families respond to trauma in different ways and frequently the methods of emotional expression and denial flip from one generation to the next. Without intervention, however, the painful effects of the unresolved trauma and the resulting denial of the identities and emotions of subsequent family members, lives on generationally. Each generation attempts to undo the pain of the previous generation.

Yael Danieli, in his long-term study of the effects of the Holocaust on subsequent generations, identified four major categories of survivor families: "Victim families, fighter families, numb families and families of those 'who have made it'." (Danieli, 1985).

The children in **victim families** responded to their parents' constant worry, fear and mistrust by remaining keenly sensitive to the pain of others, frequently entered the helping professions and, because of survival guilt, rarely let themselves enjoy success or accomplishments.

Children in **numb families** were expected to grow up on their own, seeking nurturance from others in the outside world. These adult children, because of their own needs to be nurtured, often expect from spouses that which was denied and that which they did not have in their childhoods.

Fighter families encouraged aggression in their children. They did not allow weakness, illness or self-pity. As a result, their children often had difficulty sharing responsibility and frequently sought out danger in their own lives.

The ambitions of the parents in **the families who made it** passed this on to the children. The families tended to deny the effects of the concentration camp experience and focus energy towards success in the new world. These survivors tended to marry nonsurvivors. Often the parents emotionally neglected their children with the exception of pushing them toward success. (Danieli, 1985). The parents in "the families who made it . . . tended to unconsciously encourage semidelinquent behavior in their adolescent children, using their money or position to rescue them from the consequences." (Danieli, 1985). It was as if in this case, the parents were repeating some of the elements of the Holocaust experience by unconsciously rescuing themselves over and over again.

Children of families of trauma rarely pick up messages of pain, past trauma or, like Ruth, real expectations in any direct way. They learn how to respond, live their lives and form their new families indirectly.

One man, the child of immigrant parents, explained it this way, "My mother never talked about her experiences in the old country but I knew she suffered. I learned not to burden her with my own needs or feelings. I used to hear her sigh and rattle pans in the kitchen. She never said a word, but I knew that she was hurt. I was guilty somehow. There wasn't anything I could do to make her feel better. I learned to mistrust a lot of the people in the new world, but if I wanted to succeed, I had to become like them. I learned not to feel too good, too successful.

"When I married and started my own family, I felt overburdened by the responsibility for everyone's feelings and happiness. I drove my spouse crazy trying to take care of everything so as not to upset anyone. I could only feel at peace when I was completely alone. It was the only time I didn't feel guilty. All this I learned from my mother without one word passing between us."

S. A. Harris

FIVE

Dimestores, Bakeries, Businesses And Bingo

"She and my father were oddly matched. Their life together was a 30-year war. The only prisoners they could take were children. But there were many treaties and bills, conferences and armistices signed before we could assess the carnage of that war. This was our life, our destiny, our childhood."

Pat Conroy, *The Prince of Tides*

Airport Little Girl

I saw the little girl lying on the seat between two adults in the busy airport waiting room. She was somewhere between 15 and 18 months old. Because of her youth, it was clear that one of the two adults (perhaps both) seated next to her was her parent. Each was turned slightly away from her as if not laying claim to her or each other.

121

She was sucking on a baby bottle that had been tenuously propped up against the chair. Now and again the child would pull her arms back, snapping the nipple out of her mouth, yet continuing to hold the bottle tightly in her hands. At one point a stranger, attempting to balance too much baggage, bumped the child with his garment bag. Startled, she began to cry. The man and woman, seated to either side, glanced at the child. The woman abruptly forced the baby bottle back into her mouth. "Shh!" The woman, now recognizable as her mother, said with irritation, "Eat!"

It became clear as time passed, that both individuals were the little girl's parents. They took turns responding to her occasional cries by forcing the bottle back into her mouth. It was obvious that they desired little contact with each other. The tension between them indicated a cold war of some duration. They barely spoke. When they were forced to communicate, reality issues prevailed (such as who would watch the child while one or the other went to the coffee shop, magazine stand or rest room). They would communicate in short brisk sentences. Carefully they avoided eye contact with each other or their child. At one point the little girl sat up, knocking the bottle to the floor. She reached up for her mother and was picked up with quick irritated movements. Her mother then pushed her back into a reclining position, retrieved the bottle and shoved it back in the toddler's mouth. "Shh! Eat! Sleep!"

As I watched, I observed that at least on this day, in loudly ignoring each other, these parents were also disavowing their child. It was as if they felt that she, by some intolerable quirk of fate, represented a historical link between them that neither could accept. It was also apparent as I watched over a span of an hour and a half that the tone of this day was not unusual in this little girl's life. She too readily accepted the bottle, then the cookies and crackers, as replacement for physical touch and emotional nurturing.

At one point, I wanted to intervene, perhaps saying "Excuse me. I'd like to introduce each of you to this beautiful little girl of yours," or "Pardon me. Do you know that a child requires more of you than food and clothing?" Yet, there is no court in America that would accuse these parents of abuse or neglect. The child was clean, well fed, kept safe, tolerated and not battered or bruised. Only the discarded self inside seemed to hunger, crave, cry out for emotional feeding.

Overeating

This child was experiencing the training ground for compulsive overeating. It would be no surprise if this little girl at the age of five or six would not be able to tell the difference between normal emotions, such as anger, sadness or loneliness, and the desire to eat. Food for her was becoming the replacement for emotional nurturing. Through this training she may learn to feel physical hunger in place of emotional need. It would not be unusual to find that at age 30 her most intimate friendships are with cookies and chocolate cake or that ice cream has historically staved off loneliness. A pepperoni pizza may have been the long-time ticket to reducing shame or anger. We might also see in her history hundreds of failed diets. After each unsuccessful attempt at dieting, she may have felt extreme shame, a sense of failure that was temporarily soothed by peanut butter crackers.

If overweight, she may have felt the lifelong pain of the stigma our culture affords toward "fat," started countless weight-loss programs, felt more deprivation, eaten more pizza and felt more shame and failure.

She may instead become one of the many compulsive overeaters who possess a metabolism that burns up calories and have become a thin person who focuses on the next chocolate bar as a replacement for building intimacy in relationships.

Given the experience of the little girl in the airport, it is not surprising that diets rarely work. If a double cheeseburger and fries are the only things that stand between a self and the experience of deprivation, isolation and loneliness, imagine the feelings of emptiness when those nurturing objects are withheld. It is no wonder that food is hidden, cherished and frequently becomes the focal point of life for thousands of individuals whose true self was neglected in the earliest stages of life.

Many compulsive overeaters received clear nonverbal parental messages in early life that, "Your existence is an intrusion in my life," or "You are too much for us to handle," or "If it wasn't for you . . ."

For some, however, the early substitution of food for emotional needs was for different reasons. Many parents who experienced the death of a child prior to the birth of a second child never grieved the first child's death. Frequently there were tremendous feelings of guilt regarding the death, and the next child's birth was met with ambivalence and fear. Feeding became the desperate symbol for survival. Earlier ungrieved loss prevented true emotional bonding between the parent and their living child. For some parents (who suffered early deprivation due to extreme poverty, losses in immigration or financial losses during Depression years), feeding, weight and "fat" in their children became symbols of hope and new stability. Ungrieved fears and past childhood deprivation promotes feeding their own starving child inside rather than bonding to their birth child.

Some parents who experienced emotional abuse and neglect in their childhoods fear the parenting of their children. Extremely poor self-images and internalized feelings of failure result in a lack of trust in their parental skills and an inability to bond to their child. Frequently lack of confidence as a parent leads to "parenting by the book." Elaborate schedules worked out for feeding and holding result in the clock superseding the real needs of the child. The child does not learn to experience his own hunger or emotional needs. Hungry or not, feeding time is 5, 8, 11, 2, 5 and 9. The child not only feels the parent's extreme anxiety and feels that he is "too much," but never learns to experience hunger or self needs.

These examples have in common the replacement of the child's needs for those of the parent. Early bonding, two-way communication, spontaneous interaction, loving holding, comforting and warmth are replaced by schedules, overfeeding, toys or objects, "the book" and the parent's ambivalence, unexpressed grief and terror of dependency.

Compulsive behaviors, such as overeating, gambling, spending, workaholism, relationship addictions, bulimia, shoplifting, hoarding and anorexia, are born from feelings of intense cravings for nurturing, affection and personal power. Under the surface of compulsive behavior exists an anxious discarded child crying out in loneliness, isolation, helplessness, fear and anger. Compulsive behaviors represent the child's attempt at survival, security, satisfaction, identity and safety. Each compulsion symbolizes, as exemplified by the toddler in the airport waiting room, an attempt at survival at one or more stages of development in traumatic families. The compulsions become a replacement for nurturing, expression of feelings, self-control, self-worth or security. Compulsive behaviors represent the paradox of both an overwhelming desire for connectedness and true intimacy and an overwhelming fear of intimacy. The spending, hoarding, compulsive work all reflect an effort to claim a sense of self, as well as to serve as protection against feeling the helplessness and unresolved grief of lifelong unmet needs and tremendous neglect to the true self. Like the old cartoon where an object is pounded into one part of the lawn only to pop up in another, behavioral approaches designed for ridding an individual of one compulsion frequently result in another taking its place.

Shoplifting

These attempts at "treating the symptom" fail to take into account the pain, gnawing emptiness, helplessness, fear and unexpressed anger of the neglected, discarded, internal child. Frequently childhood symptoms such as overeating, shoplifting and perfectionism are indicators of an emotionally neglected, anxious, depressed child.

Colleen

Colleen was 44 years old when she came into treatment. At that time she was the head of a large corporation and an acknowledged leader in her community. She had referred herself for treatment after being caught shoplifting. Because of her outstanding community reputation and a good relationship with the store owner, Colleen was not arrested. Her shame was intense and she felt out of control. Colleen was a single parent of three children, and the shoplifting incident occurred when her eldest daughter left home for college. However, Colleen made no connection between the shoplifting, her current loss and the feelings that were stimulated regarding herself at age 19.

Colleen originally described her childhood as being typical. Further inquiry, however, revealed that she had been an extremely intense child, a young adolescent driven toward achievement and the need to be perfect. She was the eldest of three with two younger brothers. She described everyone as "close, almost too close," except Dad who was always working. According to Colleen, her mother always sacrificed for the kids, such as saving her allowance for the children; letting them know, however, that these sacrifices had been made at a cost to herself.

Colleen: She always made sure I was dressed right, looked right. It was important to her. She said if she'd had more as a child, she would have had a much happier life. She always said she wanted me to be somebody.

Middelton-Moz: What did it mean to 'be somebody'?

Colleen: I don't know. I don't think I ever made it in her eyes. I don't think I ever did things quite right. I was just a little off. My nose was too big, I wasn't slim enough or didn't dress quite right. I always wanted to please her. I wanted her to be happy, but she never was, still isn't. I only wanted her to be happy, you know.

Middelton-Moz: What was it like for you when you left home?

Colleen: I was terrified. It all seemed overwhelming. Mom had always done everything. She even did my homework sometimes. There was so much pressure to do well, do it right. Even the guys I picked weren't right. She always said I could do better. My husband wasn't even good enough for me, or maybe for her.

Colleen got straight A's in school but felt it wasn't good enough. She always felt that her mother had favored her brothers, that they had seemed all right just the way they were. She had a nose operation when she was 21 and at that time started overeating and vomiting. "It was almost uncontrollable. I'd diet, trying to be just the right size. I'd lose control and start eating everything in sight. I'd even hide food. Then I'd make myself throw up. My days were centered around eating and vomiting."

Colleen met her husband in graduate school. He was a lawyer. She thought about him night and day. He seemed perfect. Her grades dropped some but she still got her M.B.A. with top honors.

She got married right after her graduate school. He didn't want her to work so she stayed home. Her bulimia subsided but she started to drink.

"I was so alone. I was afraid to go out even though we belonged to the best clubs. It was like alcohol made it all better. It seemed to keep me company. I always cut down when I was pregnant. It was like my body couldn't take it, but it still surprises me that my kids weren't damaged by my drinking."

When she was 34, Colleen was arrested for D.W.I. She went to an inpatient alcohol treatment center. She felt extreme shame but also some relief at being "found out." She developed relationships with women for the first time in her life through AA and felt strong enough to leave the marriage that she said had ended long before.

She started off her life as a single parent, getting her first job in the corporation where she rose to a top management position, attending AA every night. She said her life became like a whirlpool of energy.

In addition to the long hours she worked and the daily meetings she attended, she was often up until three in the morning making cookies for her children or sewing clothes for them.

"We certainly had enough money to buy things, but it was like making up to them for the time I was away. I wanted to be the best at work, a leader in AA and a perfect mother."

She did not date, did not socialize (except at work or AA) and still had occasional bouts of bulimia when things became hard at work. Eventually, she lessened her involvement in AA and began taking on leadership positions in service organizations.

"It's as if everything took on extra meaning. It began when my oldest daughter became involved in a fund-raising project for the homeless. I felt incredible despair seeing those faces in the pictures. I became an advocate for every oppressed group there was and every animal that was about to become extinct. I'd break down in tears looking at a picture of a starving or neglected child. I couldn't understand it because I was never abused."

Colleen stated that before her shoplifting incident, her life had become totally unmanageable. "I was constantly exhausted, but I never did anything normally. Everything was compulsive: my eating, my drinking, my work, the kids, social interests, dieting, shopping, everything. I've never done anything halfway."

As was the case with her earlier D.W.I., Colleen was initially relieved when her shoplifting was discovered. She was then both ashamed and perplexed.

Colleen: I don't understand it. I obviously didn't need to steal the blouse. I had plenty of money in my purse to buy it. It was strange, though. I had a similar feeling when I used to plan a bulimic episode. There was a sense of release and also a type of freedom at getting away with something.

Middelton-Moz: Did you ever shoplift as a child?

Colleen: (Initially she sat quietly as if trying to decide whether or not to speak. Then with apparent shame:) Yes, all the time. I don't know why. I could always ask my mother for things.

Middelton-Moz: How did you feel about asking your mother for, say, clothes?

Colleen: I always felt guilty, like I didn't deserve them. She always told me to let her know what I needed but I always felt that I was taking something away from her. My brothers had a different relationship with her. It was like I could never please her the way they did. What I wanted never seemed right. It was the way she looked at me, her sighs. My parents never fought. It was like a *Leave It To Beaver* household, but I knew Dad never really pleased her either. I always felt like I was supposed to make up for something, but I never knew what. Her life wasn't a happy one, but she never told me she was unhappy, just disappointed.

Middelton-Moz: Were you ever angry that your brothers seemed to be favored?

Colleen: Heavens, no! Nobody was ever angry. Besides she would say that she loved us equally. Maybe she did. It's just a feeling. She always said the right things. She was really a good mother.

Middelton-Moz: But you always felt you were making up for something?

Colleen: Yes. Like trying to please her. Once . . . this is really embarrassing . . . once, I must have been 10-years-old, I stole 15 dollars out of my dad's billfold. I went down to the store and bought my mom a teddy bear and some flowers for Easter. I wanted her to be happy. I wanted to make her happy like my brothers seemed to.

Middelton-Moz: Was she happy?

Colleen: For a while. It's funny. She never asked where I got the money. You know, wouldn't you wonder where a 10-year-old got so much money? (Colleen began to cry.)

Colleen, like so many individuals who suffer from bulimia, anorexia, workaholism and shoplifting, received a clear message from her primary parent early in life, "Make me proud. Correct my life." In that it is impossible for children to raise parents or fill their empty spaces, there is a constant feeling of inadequacy in childhood. Striving for perfection is a road without end. The real child becomes discarded early. "I am" is replaced with "I am unlovable as I am. I must try to be what you need for both of us to survive." The child feels helpless, unlovable and unworthy, and attempts to create an exterior image that will finally please the parent. The unconscious belief is that in being "good enough," "perfect enough," the parent will be pleased, become well and happy, and the child will then get parented. Unfortunately the myth never gets fulfilled and neither does the child. The child both hungers for nurturing (binge eating, relationship addiction, shoplifting, workaholism, facial surgery, compulsive spending) and feels internal rage, hungering for a sense of self and personal power (vomiting, shoplifting, self-starvation, isolation). The child attempts nurturing, release of rage and identity through compulsivity, as well as the blocking of pain and emotions. Sometimes alcohol and drug abuse also becomes an attempt at blocking the pain.

Colleen, in stealing from her father, shows a deprived child desperately in need of nurturing. She takes in anger what she feels she deserves, while also trying to create a parental system where she can finally receive nurturing and care. She takes from her father to give to her mother. In doing so, she both seeks her mother's approval and tries to repair her mother's injuries so that she can have a mom.

Compulsive behaviors, however, never lead to the sense of safety and security that is desired. The relationship sought with an addiction like hunger, once attained, is not fully accepted. If that "fantasy parent" so craved is captured, the child can never be fulfilled in a reality relationship. If the person so energetically sought is, in fact, nurturing, that nurturing cannot be accepted because the self is judged "unlovable" and "unworthy." Every word, gesture, mannerism is analyzed in light of that poor self-esteem. Jealousy and envy prevail. The person sought, who was once seen as so strong, becomes weak in light of their willingness to form a relationship.

As quoted from Groucho Marx by Janet Woititz, (1987), "How could I belong to a club that would have me as a member?" If the person is rejecting, the compulsion continues as a repetition of the original trauma in childhood.

Clothes bought on impulse are rarely "right." Food that is eaten compulsively is not enjoyed. After momentary relief, the food and the possessions become additional symbols of self-hatred and lack of control. There is never enough money saved to stave off the sense of insecurity, the fear that someday you will end up as that penniless bum or bag lady, or worse, be dependent again. The job promotion is never believed because "if they only knew . . ." The face lift is never perfect enough, and the applause never quite fills the emptiness inside. Compulsive behavior is driven by an anxious deprived angry child. There are no choices on that road and few resting places.

Colleen had little empathy for the child she had been. As those who have been allowed to glimpse her childhood, we can have great empathy for the child who was marked by internal bruises rather than external scars. We can feel compassion for her struggles, for her vain struggles, to find nurturance and identity.

After several months of therapy, Colleen was able to share that her 19-year-old daughter had been severely anorexic. "I guess in trying to achieve my own perfection, I attempted to make my daughter perfect as well. I guess I tried to use her life as some sort of proof that mine was valuable. Then I watched as she began slowly starving herself to death. It was horrible. After reading the material you gave me on bulimia, I read some on anorexia, too. It was painful to read that she needed to starve herself in an attempt to gain some small degree of control in her own life."

In Colleen's family eating disorders had traveled down three generations. Upon completing the genogram, we saw before us a grandmother who had been a compulsive overeater, a bulimic daughter and an anorexic granddaughter. The messages from primary parents were slightly different. There were injuries at different developmental stages, but the pain of an unhappy childhood existed for three generations of women. Compulsive overeaters as children frequently heard the parental message, "You are too much for me," or "You are not wanted." Bulimics might hear, "Make me proud; correct my life." Anorexics might hear, "You are part of me. You and I are one. Be perfect; be good so that we both can live."

Colleen had to be good and develop an impeccable image so that her mother could feel pride in herself. Colleen's eldest daughter was engulfed by Colleen. She needed to be a living symbol of her mother's perfection, therefore, giving up her own identity. She was not allowed to grow up or separate from her mother. Her only claim to identity was to stop eating. She then could remain in a child's body while acting out her rage toward her mother and fighting for some semblance of control by self-starvation. Her mother could force her to be good, be an image of perfection for her, but could not make her eat.

If asked about concepts of self, a compulsive overeater might reply, "I have no right to be here, to bother anyone. I am too much for people." A person suffering from bulimia might say, "I'm never good enough. I can't do anything right." A person who is anorexic might say, "I am an empty shell. I have no self. I will do what you want but will hate both of us for it."

Gambling

Individuals who gamble compulsively might make a very different statement. They might tell us that when gambling, they feel alive and excited for the first time in their life. They might tell us that their childhoods were chaotic, inconsistent, perhaps violent. They frequently were loners in the family and in life and felt very little connectedness to anyone. They also believed that they could never live up to parental images for men or women who were constantly changing. They were not tough enough, were considered "sissies" by their father figures, could not play football well enough or were not pretty enough. Perhaps they felt handicapped in childhood through illness, shyness or poverty. They frequently felt extreme neglect because of poverty, too many children, parental depression or alcoholism.

They frequently were the "lost children." Often as children they achieved their only sense of worth through imaginary friends or fantasies of greatness, pretending to be a movie star or fictional hero. Gambling not only provides an illusion of importance but frequently a network of "buddies" for the first time in an individual's life. The roller-coaster ride of expectations and disappointments frequently provides repetition of childhood experiences and traumas. The repetitious feelings are both familiar and are in themselves compulsive attempts to work through the original trauma. As with any compulsion, however, the working through does not happen in isolation and the drive towards the "next win" blocks the pain of an ungrieved childhood, of loneliness, fear and a deep sense of unworthiness which only leads to the next game. The compulsive gambler was frequently either ignored in the world of home or school, or was the projected object of a parent's self-hate. The father who cannot tolerate his own self-hate frequently gives his son all the qualities he fears and hates in himself, "If you were a man like me, instead of a weakling wimp, maybe you'd have more friends." Or,

"Why do you always disappoint me, son? You're just not tough enough."

Frequently in our attempts to treat compulsive behaviors, we isolate behaviors and ignore the internal child's pain. The gambling, the overeating, the spending are frequently seen as weakness or a sign of a lack of will, thus pointing another shaming finger at the traumatized child. Life-threatening behaviors frequently must be treated first. The anorexic needs to begin eating or will die. But, if we only treat the compulsion, we may end up with an adult who eats normally, yet becomes panicked with the smallest decision and rebels against direction while the internally starving child becomes still smaller.

Todd

Four-year-old Todd came from a home where he was "given everything." On my initial family visit to Todd's home, I found him alone in a room that looked like a luxury toy store. There was the newest of everything. Later his mother offered me cookies and coffee. Todd took four cookies and quickly hid them. The home looked like a picture out of a magazine. Everything was beautiful, neat, very clean, not a sign of childhood in any room but Todd's.

Later at the clinic I stood behind the two-way mirror painfully watching as Todd stacked toys closely around himself. Three-year-old Mary approached his wall of toys and reached for the stuffed elephant. "No, mine!" Todd proclaimed loudly. "Leave my stuff alone!" Mary walked away hitting herself as the pre-school therapist intervened.

As I watched, an observing child psychology student from a local university walked over and stood by me. "Who is that selfish little boy?" she asked casually. "Is he always so greedy? He has almost everything and still wants more. He even hoarded food at snack time."

"His name is Todd," I replied. "You're right; he has almost everything. In fact, he has everything a child would want except warmth and nurturing and someone who is able to care for him so that he can learn to care for himself."

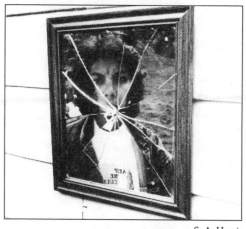

S. A. Harris

S I X

You And Me Against Me:
The Unfair Odds Of Self-Hate

A Tribute to A Native American Artist

by Jane Middelton-Moz

We'd race our horses in the summer.
He'd tell me stories
Beneath the apple trees in spring.
He made rhymes of the ABC's
That made me laugh in second grade.
He couldn't diagram sentences.
I could see animals scamper across the pages
Of the stories he'd write in fifth grade.
We said we were going to get married someday.
We'd share dreams of leaving
The sadness of our families behind us.

We dreamed of going to the fancy ivy covered colleges
We saw in books in the library.
Teachers said he was lazy, First through Sixth.
He worked two jobs every summer.
They said they passed him in school
"Cause it didn't matter anyway."
Maybe if the teachers had noticed him
He'd have learned to spell better.
He wrote love songs that made me cry in ninth grade.
He hanged himself the end of our sophomore year.
I never knew
He flunked English that year.

Many years ago I was asked to speak to a group of
Adult Children of Alcoholics in Aspen, Colorado. I
remembered being flattered by the request and slightly
uncomfortable. I had been doing a lot of speaking across
the country but somehow this was different. To me,
Aspen symbolized wealth, prestige, a place I did not
belong. I did not think about it anymore until I was on the
flight from Denver to Aspen.

Once on the plane I became extremely uncomfortable.
I noticed what everyone was wearing and I felt under-
dressed, out of place. The woman seated next to me was
dressed in a cashmere pants suit. She had given the flight
attendant a simply styled mink coat to hang up for the
duration of the flight. Feeling shy, awkward, ugly, I
scooted to the outer edge of my seat to be sure I did not
bother her. I became acutely aware of every defect I
possessed. My nose became huge. My clothes weren't
right. My hair was out of place. I felt dirty. I became more
and more distressed.

My nervousness continued to grow in proportion to
my sense of self-loathing. By the time I reached the hotel
I felt so shy that I could barely force myself to talk to the
person at the registration desk. A pleasant attractive
Swiss woman offered to take my bag and show me to my
room. I insisted on carrying my own luggage. Once in my
room, I sat in the middle of the bed staring at the

unfamiliar surroundings. Feeling small, almost childlike, I wanted to hide. I was unable to place the origin of my discomfort.

I had grown up in an alcoholic family, but I realized that what I was feeling had little relationship to the characteristics of adult children of alcoholics. I decided to take a walk and attempt to gain some control by becoming more familiar with the town.

I walked along the streets for some time. At one point, when I was browsing in a shop, a man came up behind me and said, "Don't I recognize you from somewhere?" I looked at the man, feeling even more uncomfortable, "I don't think so. This is my first trip to Aspen."

He continued to look at me questioningly, then said, "I know. You're Jane Middelton. I saw your picture up in the post office."

As humorous as it now seems, my feelings at the time were, "Oh my God, I've been found out. Everyone knows I don't belong. I've got to get out of here." I could almost visualize my picture next to the FBI's most-wanted list. Later I realized, of course, that my picture was up all over town, advertising the talk I was scheduled to give that evening. My response even at that time seemed totally irrational. However, the more the intellectual part of me attempted to gain control over my emotions, the more anxious I became. Then, much to my horror, I developed a psychosomatic symptom that had occurred only once before. My tongue swelled up and I could not speak.

I rushed back to the hotel and called a friend. My tongue was so swollen that it was difficult to relate my problem to him. Finally my friend and colleague understood. "You feel like that little kid walking down the street with your dad, don't you?" His words touched a very old and painful place and I began to cry. Through my muffled sobs I heard him say, "You know, Jane, those people you're going to talk to tonight are no different than anyone else you've talked to a hundred times. They have joys, pains and sorrows like everyone else."

I soon realized that I was feeling the intense shame my father used to convey whenever he was around "educated" or "rich folk." In many ways, I had spent my life trying to make up for my parent's shame: an attempt to undo their pain. My father had grown up extremely poor, a child of immigrant parents in the south. When he was only seven, his father died and his mother had attempted to raise seven kids by working as a sharecropper. Being one of the oldest children, Dad worked the fields with her, dropping out of school before he completed fourth grade. To help support his mother, brothers and sister, he had lied about his age and joined the Marine Corps when he was 14. He fought in World War II and the Korean War as an adolescent and young man. He became an alcoholic by the time he was barely old enough to vote.

As a child I had felt the shame of his poverty and lack of education. He never felt that he was as good as others, and I realized that my intense drive for education was for him, rather than for myself. Like him, however, I always felt "lesser than" inside. I felt like a competent imposter who would one day be found out. As a child, my father had once been denied admittance to Sunday School because he did not have shoes. He had told me many times that he had refused advancement in the military because he "was afraid they'd find out that I had difficulty with reading and numbers." My dad certainly would never have gone to Aspen and most definitely would not have put himself in the position of standing up in front of these people to speak. The child inside me felt his shame and the young woman attempted to defend against it.

Like many of the people I have worked with, I am immobilized in Aspen by shame and self-hate. Self-hate can be defined as the feeling that, "No matter what I do, I can't change the reality that who I am in the very core of my being is unacceptable in the world." This intense feeling of unworthiness is carried by thousands of people in our culture. It is frequently felt or internally defended against by cultural and ethnic minorities, immigrants to America, those raised in poverty, handicapped individuals (perceptually, physically or emotionally), those made to feel as outsiders in their homes, schools or communities, or virtually anyone whose parents or self were stigmatized as different in the broader culture.

Kaufman, in his book *Shame, The Power of Caring*, discusses the three fundamental questions that the individual, struggling with a sense of identity in a changing world, must ask himself: "Who am I, really? What is core in life for the me inside? Where do I belong?"

Stephanie

I consider similar questions when observing children or listening to adults describe difficult aspects of their lives. Once I was asked by a teacher to observe a fourth-grade child. The teacher said she sought my consultation because the child was "an extreme behavior problem." I observed Stephanie for half a day and concluded that her major problem was not a behavioral one but rather a deep sense of shame related to what I would perceive as a developmental disability. She would be calm and attentive in class until required to complete an assignment on the board or take a test. Stephanie would stare at the questions, fidget and turn her paper to different angles. I watched as her anxiety built up. As the time to complete the assignment grew short, she would begin dropping things or start throwing spit wads across the room. She would eventually be sent out of the classroom to the principal's office. In her P.E. class, I watched as Stephanie struggled to hit a ball with a bat and would miss. She would either blame the pitcher for intentionally trying to make her miss or start cracking jokes about herself.

I explained to the classroom teacher that I thought Stephanie's problem stemmed from perceptual disability and that she should be evaluated for her learning style. I was told, "You can do that if you want, but I think

Stephanie is just a naughty spoiled child. She's been difficult since the first grade."

Perceptual testing bore out my suspicions. Stephanie had severe perceptual handicaps in both gross motor and visual motor areas. The response from the teacher to the evaluation was a common one, "If she wasn't perceiving things clearly, why didn't she tell someone?" To this I replied, "How would she know that she was seeing things differently than others?"

Stephanie's label as a "hard-to-manage" child dated back to her earliest experiences. When talking to her parents, I was told that Stephanie had been considered difficult at home for as long as they could remember. She had refused to use a spoon as a toddler, was accident prone, refused to make her bed and was seen as lazy and obstinate. The parents were split on discipline and would frequently fight over what to do regarding her behavior. Her father said they were "too lenient" while her mother said her dad was "too strict."

Stephanie's mother seemed relieved, not surprised, when I began asking questions regarding her child's developmental years. She told me she had worried for many years that something was wrong with Stephanie but was afraid to confront her fears or seek help. Revealing a great deal of pain, she told me that when Stephanie had been 12 months old, she had been dropped by a sister who had been trying to carry her down a flight of stairs. The mother had been busy and had not heard Stephanie wake up. Following the fall Stephanie had thrown up and lost consciousness and had been taken immediately to the hospital.

Stephanie's mother felt responsible for the accident and was protective of her other daughter's feelings. She had been relieved when the doctor had said, "Stephanie is just fine." The accident was never discussed again by anyone in the family, and Stephanie's developmental difficulties were met with denial by both parents. Her sister felt extremely guilty about the accident but felt she could not talk to her parents about it because it would upset them. Her parents were alternately over-protective, permissive, strict and punishing toward what they perceived as Stephanie's lack of paying attention and stubbornness.

The family was anxious to talk about the accident once the evaluation had been completed. They were relieved to know that Stephanie was a highly intelligent girl who needed to be taught in a way more suitable to her learning style. They were also relieved to have her difficulties clearly stated. Unresolved grief in the family had been as profound as the guilt and denial. They needed openness, clarity and honesty to be afforded the opportunity to explore their feelings.

When I asked the pediatrician about the accident, he said, "I knew the child would have problems but I thought it best not to tell the parents. I didn't want them to know she had suffered brain trauma because I feared they would treat Stephanie differently or reject her. Also I wanted to spare the sister any feelings of guilt." I explained that I thought his lack of straightforwardness and validation had actually caused the child to suffer needless stigma, and the family's pain had grown rather than diminished in the denial. I then learned that the doctor had a brother who he felt had been rejected by their family because of a disability. The doctor, too, had suffered from delayed grief and denial.

Stephanie had learned from her parents' and sister's behavior and nonverbal communication that she was different from the rest of the family. Furthermore, she had learned that the difference was "bad." She had internalized a sense of herself as special in a negative way and saw herself as an outsider. When she moved to the broader community of school, her belief that she was different was reinforced. She could not comprehend things the other kids understood but did not know why. She took on the beliefs of her parents and teachers that she was stubborn and lazy. Like most children with undetected or ignored learning disabilities, Stephanie began acting out as a defense against being stupid.

Feeling little control over not knowing, she learned she could experience some control by acting out. She told herself that she did not care about the "stupid test" or the "dumb ball game" to protect against caring so much. The kids would laugh when she would act up or crack jokes, which allowed her at least minimal feelings of belonging.

George

George, too, had suffered from a profound sense of self-hate but for different reasons. I met him when he was 28 and had recently turned down a promotion at work, fearing he would eventually be fired for "lack of motivation." He had separated from his wife only a few weeks prior to our first session. Suffering from insomnia, he could not get to sleep until two in the morning and would wake up at four. He did not feel hungry and was "irritable" most of the time. George was severely depressed and had been for quite some time.

George: I just can't take it anymore.
Middelton-Moz: Can't take it?
George: Yeah. I'm not sure what "it" is. I guess I can't stand living with myself.
Middelton-Moz: What is it like, living with yourself?
George: Depressing. Boring. I feel like pounding on myself from the inside out. Maybe then I could make myself feel something.
Middelton-Moz: From that image, it sounds like you have a lot of feeling. What part of you is trying so desperately to be freed?
George: I don't know. I guess I never thought of it like that. (He was quiet and intense as he stared into space.) You know it's like somebody locked me up. I was just realizing, I think I've felt that way as long as I can remember, but I've just not noticed it for a long time. I remember hearing you talk about workaholism at a seminar. That's me. What did you say, "You can't touch a moving target?"

Middelton-Moz: Sounds like that child you were was pretty angry.

George: Angry? I didn't have anything to be angry about. My folks gave me everything. Everything. Things they couldn't afford. Especially my mother. She sent me to the best schools, bought me the best clothes. I even had plastic surgery on my nose when I was sixteen. She said I wouldn't get far in business with a Jewish nose. (He folded his arms tightly in front of him.) I had a nose like my dad's. Who knows what Mom's had been like? God, would you believe Dad paid for all that on a laborer's wage? Now, look at me. What a disappointment I am.

Middelton-Moz: A few minutes ago, when you were talking about the nose surgery, you folded your arms in front of you as if trying to keep something inside. What do you think you're trying to hold captive in there?

George: (Laughing for the first time) Gee, I don't know. Maybe my self.

Both of George's parents were Jewish. His father had immigrated from Russia as a young child and had learned the building trade as a craftsman from his father. George said his father frequently talked fondly of his memories as a young child growing up in one of Chicago's Jewish communities. According to George, his father said things got bad when his mother (George's grandmother) became ill with cancer. They could not afford the "fancy" hospitals and were too proud to ask for help. George's grandmother had died, and George's father and grandfather both felt responsible (even though George's father had been 11 at that time) for not providing well enough. His grandfather had died a short time later. George said that when he was a child, his father had always worked such long hours that he rarely saw him.

George's mother had been living with her family on the Northside of Chicago, a decidedly uppermiddle-class area. Her parents had frequently talked about the problems of immigration, severe ethnic prejudice and struggles to "make it" in America. Both grandparents had felt ashamed of their heritage and of their parents, who they said were "working class and very religious." Neither had returned home after they had moved out and had never wanted to align themselves with "Jews." They had instilled this value in George's mother from an early age and in their grandson, George, as well.

George had grown up feeling lonely, restricted, and confused. His mother and maternal grandparents had taught him to erase any sign of his Jewish heritage, including the features of his face. Yet his parents were Jewish. He heard stories of the embarrassment his great-grandparents had caused their children, stories that to George sounded like descriptions of his father.

He never had any brothers or sisters because his mother said, "We could only afford one child. It is our obligation to give our child the best." He was drilled in the best manners, taught to show little or no emotion because it was "lower class" to do so and sent to schools with few, if any, Jewish kids. While attending junior high school, some of the kids made fun of his "Jewish Snoz." When he told his mother about the teasing, plans were made to change it. His mother and grandparents even selected his friends, admonishing him only to pick the best and never tell them what your father does for a living. George's wife had been a neighborhood friend who was not Jewish.

George grew up trying to fit an external image created by his mother. He felt enormous guilt about the attention he received compared to the little regard given his father. He learned that who he really was, his father's son, was cause for shame. He came to know self-hate. Having learned that there was nothing he could do to make up for the "badness" behind the imposter's mask, George felt that the person he really was did not belong anywhere.

Kaufman (1980) states that there are three major external scripts that generate shame in American society. They are: "The success ethic," which requires us to compete and win by external performance standards; "the injunction to be independent and self-sufficient" and "to be popular and conform."

Consider Stephanie's chances of living up to these expectations. It was difficult for her to achieve in a school that did not recognize her learning style. She could appear independent in her acting-out behavior but certainly was not self-sufficient. Needless to say, she was not conforming to any standards of behavior.

George, on the other hand, appeared to live up to all expectations in his early 20s. He was a success by all standards, rising in a company, married to a "nice girl," appearing to be self-sufficient, popular and conforming. What happened?

As George said, "I guess the mask was just too heavy to hold up any longer."

Behind the mask, he not only hated himself, but feared that because of his Jewish roots, he could never be successful or an accepted part of family or the world. As his mother often told him, "No one will want a Jew working for their company, at least not in top management." Whether or not his mother's statements were true, he certainly got a taste of anti-semitism from his peers in junior high, as well as from his mother and grandmother. George told me he learned that many prestigious country clubs in America today will still not accept Jews. His parents had identified with the aggressor, a defense obviously born from a great deal of pain.

Ethnic Shame

It is difficult to grow up in this society as a cultural or ethnic minority, an individual with a handicap, a religious minority or a person who is poor, without feeling shame. It is impossible, however, if parents have not worked through their own trauma and shame regarding the stigma of differences in the broader culture.

Bus Scene

While riding on a city bus in New York, I observed an incident that reinforced learned helplessness and cultural self-hate. Shortly after I was seated, a Filipino child and his father entered the bus. The man was having difficulty figuring out the dollar bill changing device that was hooked to the coin slot. I was not surprised because I had experienced difficulty with it only moments before. This man, who obviously could not speak English, kept trying to put the dollar bill in the wrong slot. When he gestured for the bus driver to help him, the driver sighed loudly then yelled, "Just put it in, damn it!" The man looked more and more helpless as the bus driver continued to refuse to assist him. Finally, the little boy stepped in front of his father and looked intently at the driver, "He needs your help." The bus driver snatched the bill out of the man's hand, then screamed at the little boy, "God damn you people. If you live in this country you've got to learn. Sit down, damn it. He can't even speak English for God's sake." As they walked to a seat, the driver continued to talk loudly to himself about "these people." The little boy, who looked much older than his five or six years, kept trying to comfort his father, while the man could only stare sadly out the window, seemingly frozen with helplessness and intense shame.

Dan Dodson said it well in *Power as a Dimension of Education.* "It is impossible for a youth who is a member of a group which is powerless in the community to grow to maturity without some trauma to his perception of himself because of the compromised position of his group in communal life." He further states that as a result of this trauma, children often develop apathy, low levels of aspiration and a sense of low self-worth.

I have found that many of these children live much of their lives attempting to undo the tragic, unresolved pain of their parents' lives. Frequently parents depend on their children to interpret the language and culture, thus creating a reversal of roles between parents and children. Many as adults have talked about experiencing tremendous guilt (survival guilt) over their own success because of the difficult and painful lives of their parents. They tend to suppress their own feelings for fear of further burdening their parents' lives.

One Native American woman said, "I remember feeling the pain of prejudice early. On the school bus other kids would tease me about being a 'dumb Indian'. I couldn't talk to my parents about it when I got home because I knew they had the same pain. I didn't want to add to it. I just dropped out of school. It was never talked about." (Middelton-Moz and Fedrid).

Because of feeling embarrassed over parental encounters with the mainstream and the fact that there exist few powerful role models from their own culture, minority children frequently develop feelings of inadequacy and self-hatred. Many individuals who had parents who were ill, disabled or different from the mainstream (particularly when those differences were not openly discussed) never brought other kids home from school. They were embarrassed by their parents' behavior, dress, language or cultural values. They learned to be successful in the world of community or school but could never really integrate that feeling of success because of intense shame regarding who they really were.

Many children, who have cultivated the sense of themselves that nothing they can do will change the fact that deep down they are bad, develop a posture toward their lives called *learned helplessness*. They suffer from a sense of prolonged powerlessness.

Frequently they feel that nothing they have ever attempted has made a difference. Their motivation is impaired, often leading to the development of a resourceless stance in life. They become unable to see when change is possible. Many suffer from constant depression or intense, free-floating anxiety. Others state they have "just felt numb" all their lives.

Discrimination Of The Disabled

There were two individuals I knew in college who greatly affected my life. Both suffered blindness from birth. One young woman, who became a good friend, talked openly about her struggles throughout life. Particularly troublesome to her was to have been treated as handicapped by people in the broader world.

"Instead of being treated like a person with no sight, many people have treated me as if my whole being was handicapped. Some people would ignore me like a dirty spot on the wall they didn't want to see. Worse than that, though, were the people who treated me like I didn't have a brain or arms or legs, or like I was an infant. I remember some teachers who would talk to me as if I were not only without sight, but without intelligence or personality as well. It felt like working with me was somehow their good deed for the day. I think those who ignored me were actually more respectful, although I didn't like it. I'm sure I would have grown up hating myself if it weren't for my family. I used to come home crying or in a rage, and they'd let me talk and get my feelings out. They treated me like a normal child and expected me to live up to my full potential as a human being."

This woman's self-esteem was extremely high. Most of us in the dorm did not see her as "blind." Her openness taught us a lot. If she did need help at times, she would ask directly. She engaged in all school activities and frequently tutored others who were having difficulty in their classes. She used to say jokingly to those of us in psychology, "God save me from social workers. Don't ever become 'caretakers' of others. Please, just care."

The other individual had become "disabled" by his lack of sight, or rather, by his family's response to his blindness. He frequently spoke of himself as being disabled. His feelings reflected a high degree of self-loathing and contempt. He required assistance constantly, even to get to meals or to classes, and had to be read to for every class. He had felt totally dependent and victimized since birth. In observing his interactions with his family members, his feelings of helplessness and self-hatred became quite understandable. His parents and siblings were disrespectfully permissive and approached him with quiet guilty contempt. They did not hug him or display any loving warmth and touched him only to help him walk from place to place. He would fly into rages in their presence, which only seemed to increase their permissive behavior. It was as though members of his family had never grieved his blindness and therefore were unable to bond to him as a loved and respected self.

He once said to me, "My family members see me as a burden. I know that. I can feel it. All I've ever been is something to contend with. That's all I am now. I wish I'd never been born. I've just caused others pain and misery."

Children, in order to grow into healthy and productive adults, need to feel valued first by their parents and then by the broader community during their developmental years. They need to be shown in words and behavior that they belong. They also need to know that they are valued in their families and communities for the contributions they make and for the feelings they possess. If a child feels unworthy in the core of his being because of needs, emotions, race, financial background or contribution, he will eventually internalize feelings of shame and self-hate.

In order to survive, children must defend against feelings of inadequacy and isolation. Some children overcompensate for deeply felt internal shame by striving toward perfection in all things. Like George, they create images of competency, perfection and strength to the world.

A woman who suffered neglect and poverty early in her childhood told me she used to dip her shoe laces in white shoe polish to try to copy the "whiteness" of the other children's laces. The shoe polish and other compulsive attempts at perfection never eased her deeply felt belief that no matter what she did, she would never be as good as the other children she watched on the playground.

Cultural Self-Loathing

Some individuals, like George's mother, identify with the aggressor. They attempt to hide their backgrounds in the hostile mainstream culture and actually treat others who are like themselves with contempt and hostility.

One of the saddest parts of the rapid development of low self-esteem among native populations, for instance, has been an increasing tendency of Native American people to devalue each other. The feeling expressed by many individuals has been that if they became educated and applied for jobs in their own villages or reservations, they would not be hired because they were native.

One woman said, "Natives prefer non-natives of equal education because we have learned to believe they do a better job than our own people. We don't value ourselves. I don't understand that." (Middelton-Moz, 1986).

There are many expectations of the majority culture that Indian children will face as they move into the broader world. It will be unlikely that they will be able to attain them without denying their own culture. Competition, success and independence are not Native values. In a traditional Native home children will be taught lessons of modeling, cooperation, interdependence and the value of silence. They will also learn that the community is of greater important than independence. It will be difficult for these children to bridge these differences. If they learn statistics in school that imply that Indians are alcoholic, lazy or die early, their images of themselves will be affected, particularly if their pain is not validated at home.

Many individuals of racial and ethnic minority leave their communities to seek higher education and upon their return are rejected by their own people as outsiders who think they're better than everybody else. Frequently these individuals feel rejected by both cultures and suffer stigma in both worlds.

Some individuals, like Stephanie and my college acquaintance, stop trying. They place themselves in positions of dependency or turn to acting-out behavior as a way of both getting attention and gaining control. Some build a wall of rage, attempting to protect themselves from further shame. They may function on reversal, stating that they don't need what the world offers or no longer care. It is common for individuals who feel self-hate to turn away from friendships and intimate relationships. They may achieve success at work, yet live in isolation.

"Relationships just don't work for me," said one woman who had never been in an intimate relationship and had only superficial friendships. "I'm not a very interesting person. I'm not good for people."

Others may protect the self by demeaning themselves and focusing on the needs and wishes of others. Everyone else is seen as more worthwhile. One gentleman, paralyzed from the waist down as the result of an injury sustained as an infant, entertained others by making fun of himself. He said that he had felt as though he had leprosy as a child. He explained that his parents had talked *at* him, instead of *to* him. Possessing an extreme drive for success and risk-taking, he said he learned early that, "if I made fun of myself before others could, I'd have control over the pain."

Children who suffer stigma and prejudice regarding differences in cultural background, ethnicity, perception or economic status need not suffer the pain of self-hate. They do need caring people in their lives who are willing to validate their experiences, listen to their joys, pains, accomplishments, fears and mistakes. They need adults who have resolved their own traumas and, therefore, can teach them skills in facing the prejudices and roadblocks that frequently exist in the society in which we live. When treated with care and esteem, these children will develop pride in themselves rather than shame; internal feelings of self-respect rather than self-hate.

Walk A Little Plainer, Mommy
*Unknown Author

WALK A LITTLE PLAINER, MOMMY
said a little girl so frail,
I'M FOLLOWING IN YOUR FOOTSTEPS
and I do not want to fail.
SOMETIMES YOUR STEPS ARE VERY PLAIN
sometimes they're hard to see,
SO WALK A LITTLE PLAINER, MOMMY,
for you are leading me.
I KNOW THAT ONCE YOU WALKED THOSE WAYS
many years ago
AND WHAT YOU DID ALONG THE WAY
I'd really like to know.
FOR SOMETIMES WHEN I'M TEMPTED
I don't know what to do.
SO WALK A LITTLE PLAINER, MOMMY,
for I must follow you.
SOME DAY WHEN I'M GROWN UP
you are like I want to be.
THEN, I WILL HAVE A LITTLE GIRL
who will want to follow me,
AND I WOULD LIKE TO LEAD HER RIGHT
and help her to be true,
SO WALK A LITTLE PLAINER, MOMMY
for I must follow you.

---

*This poem appeared in the April, 1988, issue of *Healing Our Hearts*, Seattle Indian Health Board, Indian Alcohol Prevention Team Project Newsletter. Unfortunately, attempts to find the author were unsuccessful.

S. A. Harris

S E V E N

From Legacy To Choice

The Child's Eyes

by Nanci Presley-Holley

The wonder
the awe
of seeing
the world
in focus for the first time.

There truly is
every imaginable color
in the spectrum.
Not just white, grey and black
and lighter or darker shades
of those three.

Trees really do have shape
and each one seems to touch the sky.
The river isn't really a dull color
but a myriad of sparkles and shines.
Purples, greens, blues!
Even the brown grass
Has beauty in it.

I have been looking
through a dirty and cracked windshield
since infancy.
It has distorted
and marred my child's vision
since before she can remember.

I eat to nourish my body
I feel to nurture my child.
It is healthy to cry and be held.
I have worth!
Validity
and a right to life!

I am a compilation
of all my experiences
good and bad.
And I am a worthwhile person.
Glad to be here.
Happy to be a woman.
I don't have to hurry
And my needs are okay with me.

I am seeing through my child's eyes
. . . for the first time.
I looked in the mirror
and she peeked out.
I saw light and beauty.
And most of all
a friend within.

Sandra and Paul

Paul was sitting on the sofa with his arms around Sandra. He was comforting her, supporting her. Their therapy was in the final stages. My role in the sessions had changed from active guidance, clarification and interpretation, to one of support for their own healthy process.

Sandra: Thank you for holding me. This has been the nicest Christmas season we've ever had. Now I know why I got upset in the toy store today. It's hard to believe that stuffed monkey could have triggered all this.

Paul: (Giving Sandra a kiss on the forehead) I'm glad we decided to buy him and give him a good home.

Sandra: Yeah. What do you think Julie will think of Mom having her own stuffed animal?

Paul: I imagine she'll think it's pretty wonderful. She told me this was "the best Christmas ever!"

Sandra: I think it's the first time I haven't criticized the way she puts the balls on the tree. I was really awful to her. I think she's spent half of every holiday season in her room since she was old enough to help. (Her eyes teared again.)

Paul: We were both pretty rotten to her.

(They comforted each other in silence.)

Middelton-Moz: And to yourselves. It's too bad those kids you were didn't have parents who could risk making the changes both of you have. You have given Julie a gift that wasn't given to you.

Paul and Sandra had worked hard in therapy. They had originally come in to seek help for their daughter, Julie, who they saw as the problem. Julie was six and school phobic. They blamed each other for her problems. The first session had been spent acting out the pain of their childhoods in their marriage. They had threatened each other with divorce since the beginning of the marriage. When Julie was born, she became triangulated between them. From the time she could talk, she was expected to carry messages between parents who would not talk to each other for days on end.

Each Christmas season had been a nightmare. Sandra never stopped moving from Thanksgiving on. Everything had to be perfect! When Julie or Paul would attempt to help with the tree, she would either follow behind them, moving ornaments to the "right" location, or openly criticize their choices. She would finally become so anxious that she would break down in tears. At that point Paul would start screaming at her for crying and leave the room. Sandra would run to her bedroom and slam the door. Julie would be left alone by the tree. The little child would spend the rest of the day trying to make each of her parents feel better and attempt to talk them into making up.

Christmas day would be spent in a similar fashion. Sandra would work from morning to night compulsively picking up wrapping paper, cleaning and cooking a gourmet dinner. She would not let anyone help. Julie would feel "bad 'cause Mommy worked so hard and didn't even get to open all her presents." Paul would scream about Sandra's "moodiness" and "control." No one would be talking by the time dinner was served. Each would pick at the food, and Sandra would leave the table crying because "no one liked the dinner I had slaved over." Paul would leave the house slamming all the doors, leaving Julie sitting alone at the table.

Early in our work together, there was little spontaneity in the sessions. Sandra and Paul were living out the painful legacies of at least two generations. Their conversations and fights were rigid. Sides were clearly drawn as if they were each fighting for their lives. Both sides tallied the points of every battle or skirmish. Warmth and support had been held hostage in this never-ending war. Truces were signed now and again, but neither side was willing to work through and disarm the endless lists of injuries they had suffered at the hands of the other. The cumulative lists became the weapons used in each new battle. Each suffered from the belief that there were no choices. Lack of choice is the crippling injury suffered by adults who had long ago discarded themselves.

Today's session had been characteristic of the last several times we had met. There was an atmosphere of warmth, cooperation, support, openness and willingness to resolve conflict. Each could now listen to the other without sitting in terror that dropping defenses would ultimately mean loss of self. They no longer seemed to view the other as "the enemy." In their new ability to feel grief spontaneously rather than defend against the pain, they were showing compassion rather than contempt for the children they had been.

Paul: I'm sorry I was irritable, Sandra, but it seemed like old times. I felt abandoned, I guess, when you left me standing in the middle of the toy store like that. I had no idea what was wrong. I didn't know where you had gone or when you were coming back.

Middelton-Moz: Was it an old pain, Paul?

Paul: (Beginning to cry) Yeah. I felt like that little boy again, watching Mom being taken to the hospital. I never knew when or if she'd be back. No one ever told me anything. I'd feel like I had to be strong for my little sisters. Sometimes it would be a long time before Aunt Jo would come. I was so scared and then I was ashamed for being afraid. God, I always felt like the man of the house. It happened almost every holiday. It always started with Mom crying.

Sandra and Paul had stopped at a toy store on their way to the session. Sandra had burst into tears in the stuffed animal section and had left the store without telling Paul what was happening. He later found her waiting in the car. Paul had felt an old anger; Sandra, intense pain. They did not talk on the way to the session.

Sandra: (Reaching for Paul's hand) I'm sorry, Paul. I don't know what happened. It was that big stuffed white monkey in tennis shoes with the banana in its hand. (She began to cry again.)

Paul: A monkey?

Sandra: (Between sobs) Yeah, the big white one. It's just like the one I bought my mother when I was a little kid. I think I was ten. We were on our way to a family reunion in Boston. I saw it sitting up on a big shelf in the train station in Chicago. I wanted to get it for Mom. She loved stuffed animals. I spent all the trip money I had saved just to buy it. God, I just wanted her to love me like she did my brother. I used to buy her presents on my birthday to thank her for having me. (She began to sob again. Paul put his arm around her and held her while she cried.) I'm sorry, Paul, this is so stupid.

Paul: It's not stupid, honey. It's not stupid at all.

Sandra: That monkey was almost as big as I was. Anyway my parents hadn't been drinking for a few months and I was so happy. They started again that night in our compartment on the train. I guess that's where they were in the station, in the bar. My brother and I were supposed to get a hot dog or something and then go back to the train. My brother and I got on the wrong car. We were lost. All the cars looked alike. I dragged the monkey through the train. We finally found our compartment but Mom and Dad weren't back yet. I hid the monkey so it would be a surprise. When the whistle blew, we were terrified that Mom and Dad had missed the train, but they finally came in. I saw the bottle of scotch. Dad poured them a drink. I ran and got the monkey from its hiding place and sat it on Mom's lap. I was so excited. (She cried a little louder.) Mom threw it off her lap onto the floor shouting, "What in the hell is this stupid thing? I can't trust you for five minutes, can I? Did you steal this? You did, didn't you?" I told her, "No, I spent my trip money on him. He's your present." She said, "You're so stupid. What do I want with that thing? I suppose I'm gonna have to lug it around with me the whole trip."

Paul: (Hugging Sandra for a long while as she cried)

What ever happened to the monkey?

Sandra: Oh, he was left on the train.

Paul: No wonder you always apologize so much for the presents you buy Julie and me for Christmas. You can't even watch us open them. That's so sad.

Sandra: Yeah, I guess. I had no idea I had so much pain around that silly monkey.

Paul: You know what I'd like to do on the way home? I'd like us to go back to the toy store and get that monkey for that little girl.

Sandra: I don't need the monkey. I'm a full grown woman.

Paul: Why not? I think that little girl really wanted it. I think she deserves to have a stuffed animal of her very own.

Christmas was different that year. Paul, Sandra and Julie became a family that could live spontaneously in the present, rather than remain isolated or enmeshed individuals using all their energies to just survive traumas of the past. The changes were not made without grief and struggles. As Paul and Sandra received validation and understanding of their past struggles, they began to form a temporary bond. When they each began the process of trusting a little more in themselves and each other, there was a period of even greater conflict and testing. As they began to grieve the traumas of their individual pasts, there were anger, sadness and need for space. When the family began a process of realignment, from an enmeshed triangle to an adult couple and their child, Julie temporarily grew more anxious and expressed anger and sadness. She had lost the protection of the role she had played all her life of pseudo-adult. She, too, began to grieve.

As explained by Salvador Minuchin, the child ". . . like a piece in a kaleidoscope, experiences herself in different configurations — central or peripheral, brilliant or opaque, large or small, foreground or background, and in

Figure 1. Road to Self-Recovery

Recovering Discarded Self

Normal Path To Development	*Examples of Traumatic Stimuli*
Trust	War
"I am"	Poverty
"My Own Feelings"	Parental Alcoholism
"I'm Valuable"	"Learning I am of No Value"
Sexuality Exploration Separation	Parental Death
	Neglect
	Self-hate
Commitment in Relationships	Death of Brother or Sister
	Abuse
Creation of My Own Family	Abandonment

Trauma can stop normal development. Development can continue again when the trauma is faced and grieved with a counselor. Development can continue normally upon completion of grief.

each position she is circling around herself, experiencing new movements, new distances, new intensities, new silences, new words. And as her view of the other family members changed, as they exhibited more facets than they had previously shown, transformation of meaning also went on in the other family members . . . the world was no longer predictable." (Minuchin, 1984).

Julie acted out many of her feelings in play. She, like her parents, now had the four elements present in her life necessary for resolutions of grief and trauma: someone present for her, validation of traumatic events, validation of her feelings and time. She now had parents who could see her as separate from themselves and acknowledge and accept her pain. Her needs and emotions no longer threatened their own blocked pain and fragile internal identities. This family was stopping the generational cycle of pain.

When working with individuals affected by childhood trauma, I follow similar steps outlined in my first book *After the Tears*, co-authored with Lorie Dwinell. The steps in the framework, Out of Denial, Forming A Relationship, A Cognitive Life-raft, Grief, Mourning and Behavior Change, (Middelton-Moz, Dwinell, 1986) are not static but appear and reappear throughout the grief and change process in individuals and families.

Out Of Denial

Many adults and children carry the internal scars of traumatic childhood without awareness of the origins of their pain. Most blame themselves and feel intense shame for their emotions and needs. They feel they should know developmental lessons without having teachers. Many fear "being crazy," feel weak, selfish, inadequate, inherently bad and are frightened by dependency. They feel that normal emotions can actually cause injury to others. They berate themselves for panic attacks, difficulties in relationships, compulsive behaviors and procrastination. They expect themselves

to be perfect parents when they lacked parental modeling. Most of all, they deny their losses and minimize the
impact of childhood trauma on their lives.

The first step in trauma resolution is validation of
painful events and legacies. The messages to the child
are, "Yes, it did happen," "You did experience loss," "No,
you didn't make it up. You're not crazy. You're a
survivor of trauma."

Frequently three-generational genograms (family
maps) aid in the early stages of validation. When
individuals can see the legacies of trauma in their families,
it serves to validate the discarded child. Through the
genograms shown on the following two pages, Sandra
and Paul were able visually to see the pain carried on to
them from their families. They also were able visually to
see patterns that they were repeating in their lives.

Sandra, for instance, was able to see the effect of the
unresolved trauma and pain of war on future generations. Paul was able to see the impact of his brother's
death on his entire family. Both were able to see clearly
that the pain in their parents' lives did not start with
their births.

Loss histories also aid in validation, then in griefwork.
Frequently I'll ask individuals to list every loss they can
ever remember experiencing. They are asked to describe
the loss and the effect they believe that loss has had on
their lives.

One individual, for instance, remembered standing at
the window of her room looking out at her father in the
garden when a shadow passed over. The shadow was
made by a dirigible. She remembered the iron cross on
its side. She was British and it was the beginning of
World War II in Europe. The shadow in the garden
represented the loss of the world as she knew it. It
meant the loss of her innocence, homeland, lifestyle, her
safety and her father. She had never talked about it
before. She could visualize the rage on her father's face
and the fear and confusion on the face of the little girl
she had been.

Figure 7.2. Sandra's Genogram

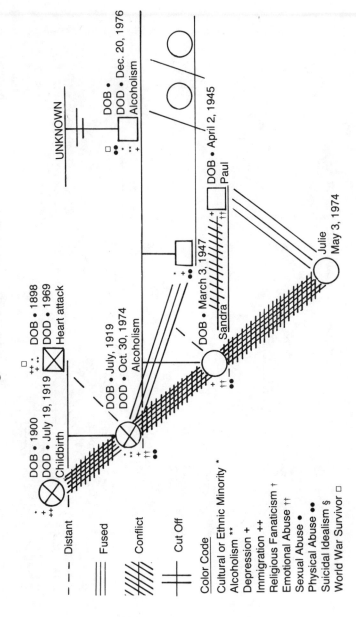

Color Code

Cultural or Ethnic Minority *
Alcoholism **
Depression +
Immigration ++
Religious Fanaticism †
Emotional Abuse ††
Sexual Abuse ●
Physical Abuse ●●
Suicidal Idealism §
World War Survivor □

- - - Distant

⫴ Fused

//// Conflict

┼┼ Cut Off

Figure 7.3 Paul's Genogram

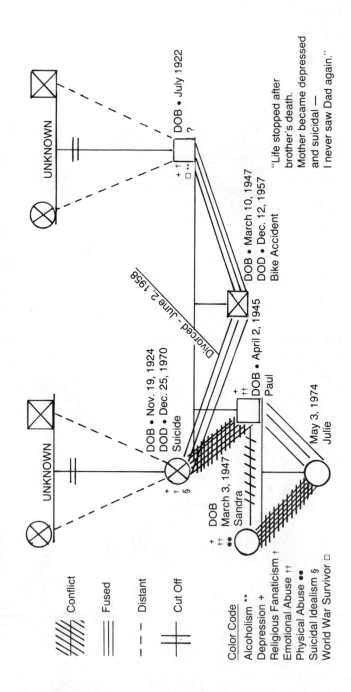

When friendships and relationships are written on the loss history, individuals are asked to write how they started, how they ended and what was felt by the child, adolescent or adult. Patterns frequently emerge.

One man listed 20 moves in his early childhood and repetitive losses of childhood friends. He could then understand the patterns that appeared in later relationships of leaving before he was left.

Many individuals may say they cannot remember losses and return with 45 pages of loss history. Some recognize how little they remember of their childhood years and can begin to grieve the loss of entire years.

Moving from denial to awareness for some individuals means coming to terms with the drug abuse and alcoholism. It is not possible to walk back through the trauma while still toxic. I recommend at least a year of sobriety and abstinence before beginning work on delayed grief.

Forming A Relationship

Individuals who suffered unresolved trauma in homes or communities find it difficult to trust in their abilities to protect themselves in relationships and, therefore, find it hard to trust others. If adults had been present for them in their childhoods, they would not be suffering from delayed grief. They would have resolved traumatic events as they occurred.

The longest and most difficult phase of delayed grief resolution is forming a relationship of trust with at least one other individual. For many, that individual is a therapist. A trusting relationship will not be formed if children or adults sense that the therapist cannot handle their feelings, particularly their anger, or has not worked through his own grief. Grief is a process that will heal itself if the individuals can trust enough to gradually drop their defenses and if the therapist can get out of the way. Frequently, individuals need to test the significant other or therapist in order to prove to themselves that these people can handle the anger, the emotions, the sadnesses that others in their lives previously could not. Often the testing comes in the form of challenging the therapist with one's anger. The internal question might be, "Can I have my feelings without hurting you or losing you?" or "Do I need to take care of you, too?"

If we consider the incredible pain suffered by the discarded child, it makes sense that forming a relationship does not come easily or quickly. There is no reason, given a childhood where no one was there, that an individual should trust without testing out that trust. Yet many survivors of childhood trauma either force themselves to stay in relationships that feel unsafe, or berate themselves for being cold, distant or defensive. Defenses were established for good reasons and are deserving of our respect.

A Cognitive Life-raft

Throughout their childhoods and adult lives, children of trauma frequently feel isolated in their experiences and emotions. The feeling of being unique, inherently bad or secretly crazy is frequently a theme in their histories. In the early stages of trauma resolution, it is important to validate the feelings of the discarded child. This period is a time of teaching and learning what it meant to have survived a childhood in a war zone or confined in an emotional ice box. A cognitive life-raft is a way to make sense out of the beginning, middle and end of the resolution process. It relieves the terrifying anxiety of being alone and not knowing a way out. It also normalizes the painful feelings, struggles for identity and necessary defenses constructed during the attempts to survive a traumatic childhood.

Cognitive understanding and validation of feelings is necessary in order for an individual to feel safe enough to risk diving into frightening emotional waters to retrieve the discarded self.

Safety and validation of feelings comes from hearing or reading, for instance, what it means to be a survivor of sexual abuse, war, neglect, emotional abuse, parental alcoholism or be a member of an ethnic or cultural minority. What are the effects of immigration on future generations? What effect is there when a child or parent dies and grief work is not completed or allowed? A problem that has existed historically in the field of psychology has been that understanding has been limited to only a few. Knowledge of child development or effects of neglect and abuse have been tucked in difficult-to-read pages of books and journals on dusty shelves of ivory tower intellectualism. What has been frequently kept a carefully hidden secret is that individuals and their attempts to gain mastery ultimately make sense.

Many workshops, books and support groups exist today that provide validation and understanding of the results of painful childhood experiences. Information and support groups exist for children of alcoholics, survivors of sexual abuse, children of dysfunctional families, survivors and children of survivors of the Holocaust. As individuals listen to or read the stories of others relating their experiences of childhood pain, addictions, panic attacks, compulsive behavior, difficulties with emotional and physical boundaries, to name a few, they frequently feel validated for the first time. As one woman said, "After a lifetime of feeling crazy, I finally realize that my painful life makes sense. For the first time ever, I realize that I'm not alone."

Many individuals, during this time, find themselves getting angry at parents or other family members. Some try to educate other family members about their pain and feel further isolated as a result. The anger or rejection during this period is frequently the individual's attempt to make a safe enough emotional boundary for the child to risk grief. As one woman told me, "I think I've dealt with my grief. I'm never going to talk to my parents again." In actuality this was only a step in the process she had constructed for safety. It was an external boundary of anger that she was using until she could develop internal emotional boundaries to protect herself from further emotional abuse. Some individuals that have been sexually or physically abused need help in constructing external boundaries to protect them from further abuse or from abusing others until they can develop internal ones. I frequently tell people I work with that *until you can feel your own boundaries, it is necessary to have rules.*

> "With the Cognitive Life-raft comes a validation on an intellectual level of the feelings of the child and a normalizing of responses that had always felt uniquely crazy."
>
> Middelton-Moz, Dwinell, 1986

When working with families, it is frequently useful to aid them in a more healthy realignment during this phase of treatment. Again as many individuals have never experienced healthy alignments in families, they will need help from the outside. During this time, I will often see the children as one unit and the parents as another. This creates an opportunity to strengthen the bonding between siblings as well as strengthening the couple's ability to communicate and parent, whether separated or living together. When the family comes back together for work as a unit, the bonding of appropriate alignments has already begun. Because many dysfunctional families tend to isolate themselves, it is important to suggest external support groups for family members to reduce the real and perceived sense of isolation they experience in the broader world.

Griefwork

Untitled

by Barbara Huston
Poor darling girl
To find you is like
Digging for a buried doll.

Some parts are broken —

Smashed, I'd say.

Lord, how it hurts
Remembering her again
This child so often killed
She finally died.

Peter wondered whether
She was there.
Was I there?

A bit is born
Not all. There's more.
Dig carefully. Go slowly.
Gently find the parts
That cry with pain
When awakened.

Grieving is a normal process in healthy families. Children grieve automatically when the event is validated, when someone is there for them and when their feelings and emotions are normalized and allowed. Unfortunately for millions of children, these simple needs are not met. Because delayed grief is multigenerational, many parents need to defend against further losses by ignoring or criticizing normal emotions in their children.

The individuals I work with, for instance, who have experienced the death of a brother or sister, frequently were never even told that the sibling had died, let alone given the support to grieve the loss. Many were told, "Joey or Tommy is in heaven now," period. Nothing more is ever said.

The parents frequently distance even more from the living child, themselves never grieving the death. In that sense, the child never dies and is a powerful ghost in the family. The remaining children have lost a brother and sister as well as their bonding to the parent. The children are never allowed to separate internally from the dead sibling. Past feelings of rivalry, normal in sibling relationships, are never resolved. This often results in these children believing that their emotions caused the brother's or sister's death. They may never allow themselves to enjoy their lives because of survival guilt. Or they may have difficulty bonding to others in their lives, including their own children, for fear of stimulating feelings regarding the original loss.

In working through delayed trauma, griefwork is the act of giving the discarded child a face. It is the process of separation. In order for griefwork to begin, there needs to be a safe environment. An individual needs to feel safe enough to allow "expression to the child of the past that experienced the trauma and develop compassion, rather than contempt for that child." (Middelton-Moz, Dwinell, 1986). Walking back through the trauma, feeling the pain, the tears, the fears that have never been expressed, is the central focus of the griefwork process. Grief cannot be processed in isolation. Children would have mastered life trauma automatically if there had been someone truly there for them.

I have often found it helpful to ask individuals to bring in pictures of themselves as children. Frequently I see compassion develop for that child when the individuals realize how small they were, that they were really just children. Sometimes I ask adult children of trauma to go to a shopping mall and watch interactions between parents and children. They are frequently surprised by the interactions they witness which provide further validation of their feelings of loss in terms of what was missing in their own families.

One gentleman told me, "I am finally realizing what 'normal' is. I think I have always somehow seen myself as an adult, even when I was three, and have held myself accountable for adult behavior. Now I know I was just a kid. For the first time, I can truly feel compassion for that child."

For some individuals, grief means being able to cry for that child for the first time. For others, letting that discarded child express his anger is at the core of the grieving process. As I frequently say to individuals, there is no right way to grieve. Sometimes an individual can cry for days over the loss of an object or a pet. Once an individual has developed a safe and caring relationship with another person and can begin to internalize that care, grieving begins automatically.

Mourning

Once the discarded self has a face and the individual has developed an ability to soothe the self and built internal boundaries, he can give a face to others in his life for the first time. Mourning is a process of integrating the past. The child must be allowed to have freedom as a separate self in order to grieve the losses of those who are no longer present.

For instance, a child who is fused to his parent will not be able to mourn that parent's death. The parent, for them, remains alive as a fused part of themselves, internally directing their movements and defenses.

A twenty-year-old woman, whose mother committed suicide, slept in the cemetery with her until someone intervened and physically carried her home. She did not eat or sleep for many days. Unfortunately no one suggested that she might be in delayed grief or supported her in working through a process of mourning. She immediately married a man whom her mother liked but whom she had previously rejected. She entered a career that had been chosen by her mother but in which she had never been interested. She became a compulsive workaholic who never allowed herself free time. She had children but could never bond to them. She constantly told stories of her perfect childhood and became depressed every year on the anniversary of her mother's death. When she reached the exact age that her mother had been when she died, on the same date and at the same time, she tried to kill herself.

This woman had never separated from her mother nor had she ever retrieved her own discarded self to integrate the past and present and mourn the death of her mother. When mourning occurs, individuals see their parents as real people for the first time, complete with strengths and imperfections. They can feel angry at the abuse or neglect and yet feel a sense of empathy for their parents' lives. They can set limits to protect themselves from further hurt without the need for complete rejection. They no longer must live in a world of rigid control in order to feel safe. Their black and white world begins to become alive with color.

Behavior Change

Frequently we expect behavior change of others or ourselves without resolving the pain of the past. This expectation is a bit like expecting a caboose to pull a train loaded with cargo up a steep hill. Yet we expect this of ourselves every time we berate ourselves for not sticking to a diet or not being able to say no to a request from another when we are already overloaded. Because we have taken an assertiveness training course does not mean that we can say no when the frightened child inside still feels the threat of abandonment. Behavior change comes with the retrieval of the discarded self.

As a therapist, for instance, I require that individuals be clean and sober for a year prior to working on grief resolution. I fully expect, however, that they will develop new compulsions and defenses in the place of the mind-altering addictions in order to protect the discarded self.

Both personally and professionally it has been my experience that behavior change occurs automatically after mourning. When we expect otherwise of ourselves or others we are heightening the messages of shame to the child. Sometimes, however, when we are at a point in our process where behavior change is comfortable, we need to learn tools for that change. For instance, persons who can now feel a sense of healthy bonding with their own children might need to read some books on child development to catch up on understanding a process that they never had modeled for them.

Native Americans, for instance, who were in boarding schools during their entire adolescence, will have difficulty understanding the behaviors of their adolescent children and how to discipline their teens appropriately.

Individuals who are terrified of water will have trouble swimming even if they have a PhD in swimming technique. After they have worked through their fears, the lessons become a necessary part of the process.

Anna's Story

In conclusion, I would like to present a story that was written by a close friend of mine, Anna Latimer. In her story, Anna beautifully portrays her process of trauma resolution. In the preface of the story, Anna thanks all of those individuals who formed the relationships with her that allowed her process to begin. In this preface she states, "I would like to thank you all for being the animals, plants, rocks and sky, and for hearing my song . . ."

"A long, long time ago . . . way before you or I were of this world, there lived on this very island, a very little girl. She was a pitiful creature for she had no home — no relations — no tribe — no anything. All the animals, plants, rocks and sky felt sorry for her. Every day they watched her wander around the island — always looking, always searching, always seeking something that she could not find. They knew that deep inside the little girl there was an empty space and this empty space needed to be filled. With great sadness, they watched the little girl wander and search. With great compassion, they reached out to help but she could not hear them. They knew that something very terrible had happened to the little girl. This terrible thing had created a great gulf between the world and the little girl.

"It seems that this little girl had come to the world uninvited. This was truly terrible for when there is no invitation, there is no welcoming. Without a welcoming, she could not be given a name and without a name, she had no beginning and without a beginning, she had no place. The little girl felt very alone. She heard nothing but her own sighs. She saw nothing but her own tracks. She felt nothing but a cold shame that began to settle deep inside her, and soon could not be dislodged.

"Slowly a weariness came upon the girl and she had great difficulty moving. Crawling along the earth, still searching she began to be filled with a white-hot rage. It burned so hot that it outlined a black and white world around her and as she reached out to this world — all that she touched burned and died. The rage turned cold as she saw the destruction and she could think of no reason to be. Turning aside and filled with an unspeakable pain, she pounded her head against the earth and began to cry. Digging her small hands into the dirt and hanging on to the earth, she cried and cried. Tears fell onto the cool, moist earth for many days. Finally she could weep no more and fell sound asleep still clutching the earth. Many days later when she woke up, she felt curiously lighter. The empty space did not hurt, and the great weariness had left her little body. Getting up from the ground, she saw to her right an old, old man. With warm, brown eyes, braids of snow-white hair and gnarled, wrinkled brown hands, he opened his arms and beckoned her to come nearer. Quietly the old man spoke,

" 'Little girl, too long you have searched for all that is already yours. By your very existence, you are the invitation and the welcome surrounds you. Your tears have cleansed your eyes and now you can see all that is around you. It is your tears that have filled the empty space with who you are. Now come and sit and listen as the world speaks your name.'

"Slowly, the little girl came towards the old man, sat near his feet and heard for the first time, the language of the animals, plants, rocks and sky.

"One at a time the animals, plants, rocks and sky uttered her name. Taking turns, they told her of her importance; they told her of her kindness, and they told her of her people. They told her of all that had come before her and all that would come after her. Their works were songs that filled what was left of the empty space with light and laughter, and the little girl for the first time laughed with the world. Filled with who she was among her people, she began to sing. It was the almost forgotten but very ancient song of gratitude. Deep down in her very own heart, she knew that this was right. She knew that all that had happened had brought her to this place, and she sang her song louder as the feeling of coming home grew in her heart."

BIBLIOGRAPHY

Abramovitch, H., "There are no Words: Two Greek-Jewish Survivors of Auschwitz," in *Psychoanalytic Psychology*, Vol. 3, No. 3, Summer, 1986.

Andolfi, M., Angelo, C., Menghi, P., Nicolo-Corigliano, A.M., **Behind The Family Mask: Therapeutic Change in Rigid Family Systems,** New York: Brunner-Mazel, 1983.

Andolfi, M. and Zwerling, I., (Eds.), **Dimensions of Family Therapy.** New York: The Guilford Press, 1980.

Beck, A. T. and Emery, G., **Anxiety Disorders and Phobias,** New York: Basic Books, 1985.

Berkus, R., **To Heal Again,** Encino, Calif.: Red Rose Press, 1986.

Blane, H. T., **The Personality of the Alcoholic: Guises of Dependency,** New York: Harper & Row, 1968.

Bowlby, J., **Attachment,** New York: Basic Books, Inc., 1969.

Bowlby, J., **Separation: Anxiety and Anger,** New York: Basic Books, Inc., 1973.

Bruch, H., **Eating Disorders: Obesity, Anorexia Nervosa and the Person Within,** New York: Basic Books, Inc., 1973.

Burka, J. B., and Yuen, L.M., **Procrastination: Why You Do It, What To Do About It,** Reading, Mass.: Addison-Wesley, 1983.

Chernin, K., **The Hungry Self: Women, Eating and Identity,** New York: Harper & Row, 1985.

Conroy, P., **The Prince of Tides,** New York: Bantam Books, 1968.

Danieli, Y., "The Treatment and Prevention of Long-term Effects and Intergenerational Transmission of Victimization: A Lesson From Holocaust Survivors and Their Children," in C.R. Figley (Ed.), **Trauma and Its Wake: The Study and Treatment of Post-Traumatic Stress Disorders,** New York: Brunner-Mazel, 1985.

Davis, M., & Wallbridge, D., **Boundary and Space: An Introduction to the Work of D. W. Winnicott,** New York: Brunner-Mazel, 1981.

Dodson, D. W., "Power as a Dimension of Education," in *The Journal of Educational Sociology,* Vol. 35, No. 5.

Dreikurs, R., **The Challenge of Marriage,** New York: Hawthorn Books, Inc., 1946.

Egendorf, A., **Healing From the War: Trauma and Transformation After Vietnam,** Boston: Shambhala, 1986.

Enright, A. B. and Sansone, R., "Anorexia Nervosa and Bulimia: A Comparative Review," in *National Anorexic Aid Society* publication, 1984.

Erikson, E. H., **Childhood and Society,** Second Edition, New York: W. W. Norton & Co., 1963.

Figley, C. R., (Ed.), **Trauma and Its Wake: The Study and Treatment of Post-Traumatic Stress Disorders.** New York: Brunner-Mazel, 1985.

Fossum, M. A., and Mason, M. J., **Facing Shame: Families in Recovery,** New York: W. W. Norton, 1986.

Fraiberg, S. H., **The Magic Years: Understanding and Handling the Problems of Early Childhood.** New York: Charles Scribner's Sons, 1959.

Frankl, V. E., **Man's Search for Meaning: An Introduction to Logotherapy.** Third Edition. New York: Simon & Schuster, 1984.

Freud, A., "Comments on Trauma," **Psychic Trauma,** Furst, S. S., New York: Basic Books, 1967.

Freud, A., "The Ego and the Mechanisms of Defense." Vol. II, **The Writings of Anna Freud,** Revised Edition, New York: International Universities Press, 1966.

Freud, A., "Psychoanalytic Psychology of Normal Development." Vol. VIII., **The Writings of Anna Freud,** New York: International Universities Press, 1981.

Fulcher, G., "Compulsive Gambling: Manipulating the Family," in *Focus on Family*, March-April, 1986.

Furst, S. S., **Psychic Trauma,** New York: Basic Books, 1967.

Gil, E. M., **Outgrowing the Pain: A Book For and About Adults Abused as Children,** Walnut Creek, Calif.: Launch Press, 1983.

Glenn, S., **Raising Self-Reliant Children in a Self-Indulgent World,** Rockland, Calif.: Prima Publishing & Communication, 1985.

Greenacre, P., **Trauma, Growth and Personality,** New York: International Universities Press, 1952.

Gruen, A., **The Betrayal of the Self: The Fear of Autonomy in Men and Women,** New York: Grove Press, 1988.

Hirschmann, J. R., and Munter, C. H., **Overcoming Overeating: Living Free in a World of Food,** Reading, Mass.: Addison-Wesley Publishing Company, 1988.

Horney, K., **Our Inner Conflicts: A Constructive Theory of Neurosis,** New York: W. W. Norton, 1945.

Justice, B., and Justice, R., **The Broken Taboo: Sex in the Family,** New York: Human Science Press, 1979.

Kahn, M., and Masud, R., "The Concept of Cumulative Trauma," **The Psychoanalytic Study of the Child,** 18:286-306. New York: International University Press, 1968.

Kaufman, G., **Shame: The Power of Caring,** Second Edition, Cambridge, Mass.: Schenkman Publishing Co., 1985.

Kempe, R. S., and Kempe, C. H., **Child Abuse,** Cambridge, Mass.: Harvard Univ. Press, 1978.

Lawrence, M., (Ed.), **Fed Up And Hungry: Women, Oppression and Food,** New York: Peter Bedrick Books, 1987.

Lukas, C., and Seiden, H. M., **Silent Grief: Living in the Wake of Suicide,** New York: Charles Scribner's Sons, 1987.

Lynd, H. M., **On Shame and the Search for Identity,** New York: Science Editions, 1961.

Mahler, M. S., **On Human Symbiosis and the Vicissitudes of Individuation,** Vol. I, Infantile Psychosis, New York: International University Press, 1968.

Mahler, M. S., Pine, F., and Bergman, A., **The Psychological Birth of the Human Infant: Symbiosis and Individuation,** New York: Basic Books, 1975.

May, R., **The Meaning of Anxiety,** New York: Simon & Schuster, 1979.

Masterson, J. F., **The Real Self: A Developmental, Self and Object-Relations Approach,** New York: Brunner-Mazel, 1985.

McGoldrick, M., and Gerson, R., **Genograms in Family Assessment,** New York: W. W. Newton, 1985.

McGoldrick, M., Pearce, J. K., and Giordano, J., **Ethnicity and Family Therapy,** New York: The Guilford Press, 1982.

Middelton, J. L., "Double Stigma: Sexual Abuse Within the Alcoholic Family," in *Focus on Family*, Sept.-Oct., 1984.

Middelton, J. L., "A Pioneering Effort: Adult Children of Alcoholics Become Parents," in Focus on Family, Jan.-Feb., 1985.

Middelton-Moz, J., "The Wisdom of Elders: Working with Native American and Native Alaskan Families," in R. J. Ackerman (Ed.), **Growing in the Shadow.** Pompano Beach, Fla.: Health Communications, 1986.

Middelton-Moz, J., and Dwinell, L., **After the Tears: Reclaiming the Personal Losses of Childhood,** Pompano Beach, Fla.: Health Communications, 1986.

Middelton-Moz, J., and Fedrid, E., "The Many Faces of Grief," in *Changes*, July-Aug., 1987.

Middelton-Moz, J., and Harris, S., **Juggler In A Mirror,** Kirkland, Wash.: Arthur Ward Publishing, 1980.

Miller, A., **The Drama of the Gifted Child,** New York: Basic Books, 1981.

Millon, T., **Disorders of Personality, DSM-III, Axis-III,** New York: John Wiley, 1981.

Minuchin, S., **Families and Family Therapy,** Cambridge, Mass.: Harvard Univ. Press, 1974.

Minuchin, S. et al, **Families of the Slums,** New York: Basic Books, 1967.

Minuchin, S., **Family Kaleidoscope,** Cambridge, Mass.: Harvard Univ. Press, 1984.

Mitscherlich, A., and Mitscherlich, M., **The Inability to Mourn,** New York: Grove Press, 1975.

Montgomery, J. D., "The Return of Masochistic Behavior in the Absence of the Therapist," in *The Psychoanalytic Review,* Vol. 72, No. 3, Fall, 1985.

Mrazek, P. B., and Kempe, C. H., (Eds.), **Sexually Abused Children and Their Families,** New York: Pergamon Press, 1981.

O'Gorman, P., and Oliver-Diaz, P., **Breaking the Cycle of Addiction,** Pompano Beach, Fla.: Health Communications, 1987.

Reik, T., **Listening With the Third Ear: The Inner Experience of a Psychologist,** New York: Farrar, Straus, 1948.

Reik, T., **Curiosities of the Self: Illusions We Have About Ourselves,** New York: Farrar, Straus and Giroux, 1965.

Renvoize, J., **Incest: A Family Pattern,** London: Routledge and Kegan Paul, 1982.

Richardson, D. W., **Family Ties That Bind: A Self-help Group to Change Through Family of Origin Therapy,** Vancouver, International Self-Counsel Press, 1984.

Robertiello, R. C., and Hoguet, D., **The Wasp Mystique,** New York: Donald I. Fine, 1987.

Root, M. P. P., Fallon, P., Friedrich, W. N., **Bulimia: A Systems Approach to Treatment,** New York: W. W. Norton, 1986.

Sandler, J., "Trauma Strain and Development," **Psychic Trauma,** Furst, S. S. New York: Basic Books, 1967.

Scarf, M., **Intimate Partners: Patterns in Love and Marriage,** New York: Ballantine Books, 1987.

Seligman, M. E. P., **Helplessness: On Depression, Development and Death,** New York: W. H. Freeman, 1975.

Viorst, J., **Necessary Losses,** New York: Fawcett Gold Medal, 1986.

Waelder, R., **The Basic Theory of Psychoanalysis,** New York: International Universities Press, 1960.

Waelder, R., "Trauma and the Variety of Extraordinary Challenges," **Psychic Trauma,** Furst, S. S., New York: Basic Books, 1967.

Woititz, J. G., **Home Away From Home: The Art of Self-Sabotage,** Pompano Beach, Fla.: Health Communications, Inc., 1987.

Woititz, J. G., **Struggle for Intimacy.** Pompano Beach, Fla.: Health Communications, 1985.

Other Books By . . .

HEALTH COMMUNICATIONS, INC.

Enterprise Center
3201 Southwest 15th Street
Deerfield Beach, FL 33442
Phone: 800-851-9100

ADULT CHILDREN OF ALCOHOLICS
Janet Woititz
Over a year on The New York Times Best Seller list,this book is the primer
on Adult Children of Alcoholics.
ISBN 0-932194-15-X   **$6.95**

STRUGGLE FOR INTIMACY
Janet Woititz
Another best seller, this book gives insightful advice on learning to love
more fully.
ISBN 0-932194-25-7   **$6.95**

DAILY AFFIRMATIONS: For Adult Children of Alcoholics
Rokelle Lerner
These positive affirmations for every day of the year paint a mental picture
of your life as you choose it to be.
ISBN 0-932194-27-3   **$6.95**

*CHOICEMAKING: For Co-dependents, Adult Children and Spirituality
Seekers* — Sharon Wegscheider-Cruse
This useful book defines the problems and solves them in a positive way.
ISBN 0-932194-26-5   **$9.95**

LEARNING TO LOVE YOURSELF: Finding Your Self-Worth
Sharon Wegscheider-Cruse
"Self-worth is a choice, not a birthright", says the author as she shows us
how we can choose positive self-esteem.
ISBN 0-932194-39-7   **$7.95**

LET GO AND GROW: Recovery for Adult Children
Robert Ackerman
An in-depth study of the different characteristics of adult children of
alcoholics with guidelines for recovery.
ISBN 0-932194-51-6   **$8.95**

LOST IN THE SHUFFLE: The Co-dependent Reality
Robert Subby
A look at the unreal rules the co-dependent lives by and the way out of the
dis-eased reality.
ISBN 0-932194-45-1   **$8.95**

New Books . . .
from Health Communications

BRADSHAW ON: THE FAMILY: A Revolutionary Way of Self-Discovery
John Bradshaw
The host of the nationally televised series of the same name shows us how families can be healed and we as individuals can realize our full potential.
ISBN 0-932194-54-0   **$9.95**

HEALING THE CHILD WITHIN: Discovery and recovery for Adult Children of Dysfunctional Families — Charles Whitfield
Dr. Whitfield defines, describes and discovers how we can reach our Child Within to heal and nurture our woundedness.
ISBN 0-932194-40-0   **$8.95**

WHISKY'S SONG: An Explicit Story of Surviving in an Alcoholic Home
Mitzi Chandler
A beautiful but brutal story of growing up where violence and neglect are everyday occurrences conveys a positive message of survival and love.
ISBN 0-932194-42-7   **$6.95**

New Books on Spiritual Recovery . . .
from Health Communications

THE JOURNEY WITHIN: A Spiritual Path to Recovery
Ruth Fishel
This book will lead you from your dysfunctional beginnings to the place within where renewal occurs.
ISBN 0-932194-41-9   **$8.95**

LEARNING TO LIVE IN THE NOW: 6-Week Personal Plan To Recovery
Ruth Fishel
The author gently introduces you to the valuable healing tools of meditation, positive creative visualization and affirmations.
ISBN 0-932194-62-1   **$7.95**

GENESIS: Spirituality in Recovery for Co-dependents
by Julie D. Bowden and Herbert L. Gravitz
A self-help spiritual program for adult children of trauma, an in-depth look at "turning it over" and "letting go".
ISBN 0-932194-56-7   **$6.95**

GIFTS FOR PERSONAL GROWTH AND RECOVERY
Wayne Kritsberg
Gifts for healing which include journal writing, breathing, positioning and meditation.
ISBN 0-932194-60-5   **$6.95**

Books from . . .
Health Communications

THIRTY-TWO ELEPHANT REMINDERS: A Book of Healthy Rules
Mary M. McKee
Concise advice by 32 wise elephants whose wit and good humor will also
be appearing in a 12-step calendar and greeting cards.
ISBN 0-932194-59-1   **$3.95**

BREAKING THE CYCLE OF ADDICTION: For Adult Children of Alcoholics
Patricia O'Gorman and Philip Oliver-Diaz
For parents who were raised in addicted families, this guide teaches you
about Breaking the Cycle of Addiction from *your* parents to your children.
Must reading for any parent.
ISBN 0-932194-37-0   **$8.95**

AFTER THE TEARS: Reclaiming The Personal Losses of Childhood
Jane Middelton-Moz and Lorie Dwinnel
Your lost childhood must be grieved in order for you to recapture your
self-worth and enjoyment of life. This book will show you how.
ISBN 0-932194-36-2   **$7.95**

ADULT CHILDREN OF ALCOHOLICS SYNDROME: From Discovery to Recovery
Wayne Kritsberg
Through the Family Integration System and foundations for healing the
wounds of an alcoholic-influenced childhood are laid in this important
book.
ISBN 0-932194-30-3   **$7.95**

OTHERWISE PERFECT: People and Their Problems with Weight
Mary S. Stuart and Lynnzy Orr
This book deals with all the varieties of eating disorders, from anorexia to
obesity, and how to cope sensibly and successfully.
ISBN 0-932194-57-5   **$7.95**

Orders must be prepaid by check, money order, MasterCard or Visa.
Purchase orders from agencies accepted (attach P.O. documentation)
for billing. Net 30 days.

Minimum shipping/handling — $1.25 for orders less than $25. For
orders over $25, add 5% of total for shipping and handling. Florida
residents add 5% sales tax.

THE MAGAZINE FOR AND ABOUT . . .

ADULT CHILDREN OF ALCOHOLICS

WE UNDERSTAND. . .

. . . what it means to be the child of an alcoholic. We know the confusion, the intense self-criticism, the bottled-up anger you carry with you. You are not alone.

How do we know? Because we, like you, are part of the 28 million Americans who are children of alcoholics. And we have seen our numbers grow into a social movement focused on the special needs and understanding of people like us.

Changes . . . The Magazine For and About Children of Alcoholics, is part of the new vision of hope for CoAs everywhere. The understanding that comes from caring can lead to healing. But none of us can do it alone. We need each other. The isolation, desolation and despair of the alcoholic family is not all that binds us. It is the hope — and the truth — that things will get better.

We hope you share in the vision by subscribing to *Changes* . . . For and About Children of Alcoholics. It's a change for the better.

☐ **YES** . . . Send my subscription to the following address:
☐ 1 Year (6 Issues) . . . $18.00   ☐ 2 Years (12 Issues) . . . $34.00

Your Name: _____

Address: _____

_____

Payment Form (Check One):

☐ Check or Money Order Enclosed (Payable to The U.S. Journal)

☐ M.C. #: _____ Exp. Date: _____

☐ VISA #: _____ Exp. Date: _____

Agency P.O.'s & Vouchers accepted. Attach documentation for billing purposes.

Cardholder's Signature: _____

The U.S. Journal, Inc., 3201 S.W. 15th Street, Enterprise Center
Deerfield Beach, FL 33442 • 1-800-851-9100